Advance Praise for the Book...

"When I received *Life Force Marketing: A Prosperity Guidebook for Holistic Practitioners Who Don't Like Marketing* to review, I was struggling with direction in my own Feldenkrais practice. What a gift! Meriah's easy, conversational style is intelligent and inviting—she invites you to think about questions that you may not have thought of or you might be avoiding. But unlike many other marketing books and programs this is not a dry "how to." I didn't experience the pressure I often feel when I work with other marketers. Meriah's strategies have helped me work through my own confusion and next steps in my own practice. It's the kind of book you want to pick up periodically to check the trajectory of your business and to get inspiration. I would recommend this book to any holistic practitioner who is searching for a path forward."

Kate Pilgrim, Athens, Georgia
Guild Certified Feldenkrais Practitioner

"*Life Force Marketing* is an invaluable resource and a practical guide, a must read if you have a heart-felt mission and want to make more money doing what you truly love. It feels like Meriah is an angel on your shoulder whispering "you can do it!" as she shares a wealth of hard won wisdom in a very soulful way. Meriah generously teaches us how to share our work and spread our message in a way that feels natural and authentic. Act on what she teaches, and you can reach the potential you imagine for your business and your life."

Jan Marie Dore, Guelph, Ontario
Business Mentor to Women Coaches & Change Makers

"Meriah Kruse has written a practical and inspiring guidebook for anyone wishing to be a force for good in the world. By re-imagining the purpose of marketing to be reflective of our most noble aspirations and capacities, she makes a contribution in an area most desperately in need of a major facelift and paradigm shift: selling. If you have ever dreamed of being a person of influence or dreamed of a world that works better for everyone; this is the book for you! Thank you Meriah for this inspiring, practical, step-by-step guide!"

Russell Mariani, South Hadley, Massachusetts
Health Educator, author of *Healing Digestive Illness*

More Advance Praise for the Book...

"This book should be read by anyone looking to start their own business in the field of bodywork or other alternative creative businesses. We've needed it to be written for a long time. Having been a body therapist for 30 years and an instructor in this field for over 25, I still found this book relevant in terms of how to proceed in my life now, not only as a therapist but as a person. Meriah's personality and sense of purpose, as well as her joy for living and giving, is so apparent throughout the entire book."

Judy Gray, Albuquerque, New Mexico
Veteran body therapist and massage instructor with practices in Kentucky and New Mexico, former co-owner of Lexington Healing Arts Academy

"This book is chock full of concise, straightforward, well-presented, easy-to-follow practical how-to's. Meriah has spent years learning how to do it right and offers concrete advice so others can avoid the pitfalls and sometimes overwhelming path involved. While her extensive research and knowledge is obvious, it is her many years in holistic practice and her hands-on marketing experience that adds credence to her recommendations. Her approach reflects a deep understanding of the fears, uncertainty, and challenges, but also the excitement, involved in the process. She gently presents the steps you need to take to achieve your goals for marketing a solo business in an ethical, compassionate, heart-felt way."

Jan Gish, Lexington, Kentucky
Reiki Practitioner, former Artificial Intelligence Programmer

From the Contributing Editor:

"Meriah Kruse offers a heart-felt, holistic approach to marketing focused on the needs of the client and the vision of the practitioner. She teaches you how to align your mindset with your marketing strategy. This is a more sincere, organic form of marketing which stems from the twin goals of spreading enlightening attitudes about business, and raising the prosperity level of her fellow holistic practitioners. I highly recommend *Life Force Marketing* to any professional who promotes themselves to sell a service."

Balin Kruse- Williams
Advanced Marketing Solutions
Lexington, Kentucky

Meriah Kruse, Prosperity Marketing Coach

"Working with Meriah has been a joy! I always come from our appointments with a lighter step and a smile on my face. The meetings are full of information that would have taken me months, if not years, to figure out on my own -- and then I would have left out the most important component... MY VISION! I could go on and on about how I hate putting myself out there, but she let me know there are many ways to do that other than getting in front of a group of people. Having this book and Meriah's guidance has made all the difference in starting my own business. Thank you, Meriah Kruse." K. Erin Mills, Bluebird Massage, Lexington KY

"Meriah has an incredible ability to listen and help sort through the complex layers of a newly emerging vision; layers that involve history, new directions, strategy and the practical organization of tasks. She can also implement tasks in and around design work; her designs are beautiful and get results. Meriah also has a remarkable ability to sense when a gentle gesture of mirroring a new idea I have is needed. And she also knows when a slightly stronger suggestion is in need - such as helping me to think about how to pace myself. I feel in good hands with Meriah; I feel as if she is guiding me to "take a hand" so to speak, in my own process of rebranding and repositioning my work. I unhesitatingly recommend Meriah and Life Force Marketing." Katie Bull, vocal coach, cross-disciplinary artist, Whole Body Voice (c), New York, NY

"The whole vision of my future just opened up after only one hour of chatting with Meriah. Excited doesn't even begin to express how I feel about this beautiful journey we have embarked on of self-discovery, healing & learning how to let the people know who I AM & that I am HERE! Hanna Lee, Shamanic Bodyworker, Lexington KY

"Meriah has endless enthusiasm and has been a great support as a marketing coach. She has given me a new way of thinking about marketing as a Holistic Practitioner. She has helped me create focused strategies to reach my ideal client...and shown me the power of using plain talk instead of resumé talk and industry jargon." Franki, Health Advisor and Nurse Coach, Keene, KY

"You are one of the most interesting, informed, intuitive, healing speakers I know. When you open your mouth and speak and when you write...you always move me. You are a gifted communicator...!" Jenny, Nashville, TN

"Working with Meriah was one of the best business decisions I have made. Her kind heart and creative approach has helped me grow my business and cultivate new relationships. I wouldn't have flourished to this extent without her push!" Kalee Vicars, Pure Romance Consultant, Columbus, Ohio

MARKETING

A Prosperity Guidebook

for Holistic Practitioners Who Don't Like Marketing

~ 10 Steps to a Healthier Small Business ~

LIFE FORCE

Life Force is an unseen energy that circulates in our Universe, in us, and in all living things. My Cherokee ancestors believed that Life Force even circulates in the rocks, crystals, and minerals produced by Mother Earth.

As writer and health educator Russell Mariani puts it, "Life Force is the universal source from which all living things arise and flourish."

As such, Life Force is precious, a gift of immeasurable value. It may be constant, and yet our experience of it fluctuates in a given moment depending on how we're engaging with Life in body, mind, and spirit.

Our Life Force is something we consciously protect and amplify when we seek out inspiration or express gratitude, hug a tree or our children, cultivate unconditional love, intentionally develop our inner powers, connect with our spiritual selves, light the fires of personal creativity, or take care of ourselves and others.

I've noticed that when I follow some of the steps recommended here in our book – especially the ones with an inner focus -- I often feel more filled with and propelled by Life Force as a result. I feel more empowered, clear, joyful and serene. I've seen it work the same magic on friends, colleagues, and clients. I can't hope to fully comprehend how or why this amplification of our Life Force takes place, but I believe we can claim the capacity for ourselves. This might be our greatest reason for Gratitude.

And if we have a holistic or creative business of some kind -- a place to focus some of that Life Force in the service of others -- all the better.

I hope you'll read and think through enough of our book to experience this process for yourself. May you, and all beings, be free from suffering.

Meriah Kruse
Author, Prosperity Marketing Coach

Balin Kruse-Williams
Contributing Editor
Marketing and Crowd-funding Advisor

Erin Mills
Administrative Support

in memory of

Pam Sexton

Rhea Lehman

Lynne Maner

dear friends with so much
genius
creativity
wisdom
friendship
vision and
passion

all of which you shared freely.

Here's what I want you to know:

You are still vibrating, intensely,
in our collective minds and heart

LIFE FORCE MARKETING:
A Prosperity Guidebook for Holistic Practitioners Who Don't Like Marketing

~10 Steps to a Healthier Small Business ~

by Meriah Kruse
Balin Kruse-Williams, Contributing Editor

www.LifeForceMarketing.com

Published by New Paia Press
2314 Southview Drive
Lexington KY 40503

ISBN
978-0-692-14010-9

Cover art and interior design by Meriah Kruse
Cover based on a photo by:
Milada Vigarova, from Unsplash.com

Additional support:
Miki Wright, Egg Design
Duncan Veach, Beau Graphics
Phil Yarnall, Smay Design

Table of Contents

CHARTS and VISUAL AIDS

Acknowledgment

Teachers, colleagues and coaches who have taught me about writing, prosperity, marketing and business. In chronological order…

The late Mary Buck, my high school English teacher
Thank you for encouraging me as a writer when I was a tender age.

Dr. Linda Pannill, former Director, Kentucky Women Writers Conference
Planning and executing a marketing campaign

Orrin Wright
Impromptu crash course in prosperity and allowing my light to shine

Halifu Osumare and Katherine Kramer
Event management, program development, performing arts marketing

Zhenya Williams
Joomla, website editing, Flickr, Creative Commons, Photo-Shop

Tad Hargrave
Niche marketing, personal manifesto, tribe building

Bill Baren
Coaching, client enrollment, teleseminar production, local marketing hubs

Jan Marie Dore
Coaching, brand definition, women in business

Ryan Eliason
Coaching, Visionary Business Mastery, joint ventures, internet marketing

Unity of Louisville and Stretton Smith
4-T Prosperity Courses

Beth Wofford and Trish Schwenkler
Coaching, relationship marketing, advanced network building

Tyler Norton
Defining and adhering to an ethos in business, prosperity studies

Cardell and Linn Vermillion Smith of Quantum Life Changes
Managing personal energy in the prosperity envisioning process

Mary Morrissey
Dream building, prosperity studies, coaching, embracing a massive vision

Denise Wakeman
Visibility Training, launching a book, blogging, coaching

Thank You

I begin with thanks to Mary Morrissey, founder of Life Mastery Institute. When I first heard her ask, "Imagine the Life you would love living," something I'd been pursuing for 30 years clicked into place: The ability to actively imagine my future.

There will never be adequate opportunity to thank my mother, Carole Grace Kurtz Kruse, my most long-standing supporter. Her generosity and proud enthusiasm in the face of my schemes and visions has buoyed me a thousand times.

Kudos and appreciation to my son, marketing advisor, contributing editor and Chief Shoulder to Lean On, Balin Kruse-Williams, for his loyalty, imagination, scrupulous eye for process, work ethic, smart analysis, kindness, disturbing impersonations, and absurd sense of humor.

To Dhyani Ywahoo, my wisdom teacher, whose Diamond Body Practice taught me 35 years ago about igniting the fires of intention.

Gratitude to the late Dr. Moshe Feldenkrais, Ph.D., whom I never met, for the gifts of transformation, vocation, intellectual stimulation, a community of colleagues, and a technology of consciousness to satisfy many of my greatest curiosities.

Additional thanks to Rona Roberts, one of the best people I know, for many things, such as saying over lunch at the Good Foods Bistro, "Meriah, have you ever thought about being a coach? It seems like you naturally do that anyway."

Susan Bailey, a friend, for listening every week, for years, and egging me on with her unfailing ability to see the value in what I'm imagining.

My readers/collaborators, for reading the manuscript, commenting generously, and making this a much better book: Susan Bailey, Beth Wofford, Balin Kruse-Williams, Gene Williams, Alan Questel, and Lee Archambeault. Also, to the Carnegie Center for Literacy and Learning for maintaining a shining beacon for everyone in Central Kentucky who wants to write, publish, and be heard.

To Verdis Norton, Founder and Board President Emeritus of ASEA Cellular Health, for insisting I think beyond the confines of what seemed possible.

To all 58 of my Indiegogo crowdfunding partners -- and everyone who pre-ordered a copy of this book, without whom it wouldn't have come to pass.

And, finally, to my clients, past, present and future, whose big hearts and commitment to their prosperity visions is a continual source of inspiration, and a great reason to get out of bed every morning.

MARKETING

A Prosperity Guidebook

for Holistic Practitioners Who Don't Like Marketing

~ 10 Steps to a Healthier Small Business ~

by Meriah Kruse

introduction

Let's Start this Conversation

The Scope of Our Book

Is Our Book for You?

What is Holistic Marketing?

Tips for Using Our Book

Legend

About the Art Work

Let's start this conversation...

I have a great appreciation for holistic practitioners and creative service providers. Many have been my peers during the past 35 years: massage therapists, Feldenkrais practitioners and other movement educators, choreographers, performing artists, wellness and health coaches, energy workers, acupuncturists, art, dance and music therapists, naturopaths, and spiritual and life coaches.

I've observed that this group of people, most of whom have chosen to serve others as a livelihood-of-the-heart, are a dominant force for good in the world.

Through a lengthy process – over 35 years – of marketing myself and the companies and projects I've worked with, I've honed my knowledge of a particular approach to marketing, something that, to an extent, erupted from my own experiences.

I'm calling it 'Holistic Marketing.'

Now I've written a book in hopes of passing some of this knowledge on to you. I know you can become successful faster and more efficiently than I did. I don't want you to have to spend the many hours I did sifting through the endless library of marketing advice available online. I don't want you to suffer through years of trial and error to finally figure out what works.

I wrote this book so you can find a way of promoting your work in the world that allows you to be genuine, producing something you're proud of that's valuable to your potential clients and yourself.

Ours Is Not the Domain of Business and Greed

Do you experience a disconnect when you try to reconcile your love of people -- and the reason you got into your profession in the first place -- with the need to engage in marketing, the domain of business and greed?

By using our book as a how-to guide, you will surely arrive at a new starting point for your business. You can find yourself on the doorstep of a vibrant, intelligent, intuitive new approach to marketing yourself and your work that's aligned with your values and fits with how you naturally interact with people. You'll have enough understanding to immediately start building – or rebuilding -- the thriving holistic, integrative, or creative private practice of your dreams.

You'll see how marketing is part of your work in the world. Applying the principles of holistic marketing, knowledgably and sincerely, will help you fulfill two of the most important roles you have as a solo service provider:

1. Making yourself visible to those who need what you have to offer;

2. Speaking about your work in such a way that, when they do discover you, they'll recognize you're the person they've been looking for, the professional who can help them solve an important problem.

Your reluctance or distaste for marketing yourself will decrease, or even fade away, as you see the amount of good you're doing for others by fulfilling these two roles.

After all, what's the use of having outstanding skills,
world-class training, highly developed sensitivity,
intuition and perceptive abilities and a vast knowledge base
if no one knows you're there or how you could help them?

What to Expect? Step-by-Step Results

Step 1 ENVISION the Life you want to live
Explore a 6-step prosperity process that will serve you for a lifetime. It will point you toward a clear Vision of the Life you want to live and the work you want to do.

Step 2 REVISE the stories you tell yourself about yourself
Know how to address your inner dialogue and stay positive while you build your business, even on the days when it's not easy.

Step 3 REMEMBER your resources, a fresh way of looking at assets.
Experience a renaissance in understanding the power of your existing resources, including how they can shape the stories you tell.

Step 4 CHOOSE the people you want to serve and what to offer them.
Understand what a target audience is, why you should choose one and how to make the choice. You'll develop a new sense of clarity about your purpose.

Step 5 COMPOSE your compelling stories.
Discover the best stories you could be telling about yourself and your work and the most important people who should hear your story. You'll create your elevator speech, business name, one-minute conversation, leading questions, and a biographical statement.

Step 6 SELECT a strategy for spreading your stories.
You'll survey the marketing channels you could use to share your stories with potential clients and select the 2, 3 or 4 best ones for you. You'll learn to relax and enjoy the ride!

Step 7 BUILD your marketing infrastructure.
Know the advantages and disadvantages of building your marketing channels yourself vs. hiring someone to help. You'll learn some of the essential questions to ask when enlisting assistance.

Step 8 ENLIST others to encourage and teach you, keep you on track.
Understand the importance of having a formal or informal team behind you, and also what's reasonable to expect from different kinds of helpers.

Step 9 CONTINUE to follow-up, look forward, monitor, listen, and revise.
Delve into the long-term process of maintaining a business over time, including what to pay attention to and how to prepare.

Step 10 CELEBRATE every victory!
Come away with a deep-seated understanding that celebrating every victory is not just the cherry on top, but a commitment to yourself that will make every day more joyful.

An Expansive Vision for Holistic, Alternative, Complementary, Integrative and Creative practitioners

Although it isn't widely acknowledged, the members of our worldwide community of practitioners and artists are often the ones that people turn to for support in forging a healthier, more satisfying lifestyle. We are often the Go-To resources for people wanting to learn about holistic, alternative, complementary or integrative approaches to health and wellness, self-awareness, self-image, creativity, and self-actualization.

We practitioners are privy to the inner lives of others; in many cases, we're the only ones with whom clients share their most intimate secrets, frustrations, pain, and aspirations. More often than the general public might suspect, clients arrive on our doorsteps after they have visited doctors, therapists, and other experts – and left without the help they needed.

Often, the needed help finally arrives in the form of hands-on bodywork, a Feldenkrais or coaching session, an African Dance class, or a week-long self-empowerment retreat.

I know this from personal experience, both as a professional provider and as a recipient. I've spent countless hours in the company of creative artists and holistic practitioners who light up the world with their ideas, skill, compassion, intuition, and innovation.

REVELATIONS: My first massage therapist

She was the first massage therapist who moved me to tears. I don't remember her name, and I only saw her twice. She had a master's degree in something I'd never heard of; she was knowledgeable in massage therapy as a tool for self-discovery. Her touch, her patient inquiries and the insights she shared with me during our 2-hour sessions were a total revelation. This talented and compassionate bodyworker started me down a path that substantially altered my Life. I was living in Berkeley, California at the time when, even in the early 70's, holistic practitioners were already in high demand. I was fortunate, after growing up in conservative Kentucky, to arrive in the Bay Area at the perfect time. I discovered dedicated practitioners of homeopathy, acupuncture, herbal medicine, breath work, dance, massage, meditation and Bio-Energetics therapy, as well as consciousness technologies like Transcendental Meditation and the est training. That's how I first learned about the power of this emerging tribe of personal change agents.

My early bodywork experience in California led me to know that one day I would become a massage therapist. In the interim, and ever since, I've been promoting myself and my services ... either as a dance professional, massage therapist, Feldenkrais or Bones for Life© practitioner, marketing coach or adventure travel operator.

Is there something holding our community back from reaching its full potential, both individually and collectively? I think so.

Holistic healing artists and creative service providers are already making a positive impact in the world. Our clients are fully aware of the depth and range of our abilities. Collectively, we have a massive loyal following. However, the society at large is not aware of us; we're not on their radar. One symptom of this is that many of our businesses don't fully prosper. All too often, we don't have a steady supply of clients, and so we don't feel relaxed and prosperous in relationship to money.

I'd like to contribute to both our individual and collective impact by sharing prosperity teachings in a holistic marketing framework. I believe this can lead to more practitioners with lucrative businesses -- which means, more importantly, that millions of people who are suffering will learn about who we are and how we can help.

For many of us, marketing doesn't come naturally. To some, the whole idea of marketing and sales is distasteful. Sound familiar? Do you see marketing this way, as something that's either manipulative, crass or inappropriate for someone with a sensitive character or higher spiritual aspirations? Similarly, do you feel like many others who will gladly admit they can't stand the idea of selling? If so, you may associate marketing with coercion, with trying to talk people into doing something they don't want to do, with being pushy or sleazy.

Here lies the dilemma. No one can have a sustainable enterprise without eventually selling something to someone. You're in the marketplace even if you don't fully understand what that means or are not quite ready to embrace the idea. Perhaps you can make room for a shift in your attitude about what it means to market your services. By doing so, you can alter the reach of your work, and more fully take your place as a person of influence in a changing world that desperately needs what you have to offer.

Maybe it's time to ask... What is Marketing?

When it comes right down to it, marketing could be described very simply as a well-conceived and highly organized way of notifying the world about what you have to offer and how you can solve their problems. In his best-selling book "TRIBES," Seth Godin gives a brief definition that will influence how we talk about marketing in our book:

> "Marketing is the act of telling stories about the things we make -- stories that sell...stories that spread... It is about engaging the tribe."

The most important message I want to share with you is this: The best marketing is not coercive in any way. If your work is an expression of a heartfelt mission, the right kind of marketing will be holistic in itself! Not only is marketing a necessity, but it's also something worthy of learning about and embracing as part of your work in the world. More specifically, it's a way of telling stories to the people you want to serve, notifying them about how you can help solve their problems and alleviate their pain, whether it's physical, emotional, familial, creative or financial. This process is a part of your calling.

The greatest talents often lie buried out of sight.
Plautus

The Scope of Our Book

Although it would take an encyclopedia to cover everything you might want to know and to give you step-by-step instructions in every area related to marketing your practice, what I can do is introduce concepts that will apply to any marketing you choose and put you on the path to a prosperous professional Life.

Because marketing changes all the time, you will need to continue your education after you've read our book. Hopefully, you'll continue to learn because you'll be practicing what you've read here! In marketing, as in so many things in Life, experience is the best teacher. (I still learn something new about marketing almost every week!)

You may need to hire a marketing coach or business mentor to help you implement some of what you're learning here.

Your business is unique. While the principles presented here are useful in a wide variety of circumstances, your company may require something that's not explained in detail here.

We feel confident in promising that you'll come away from reading our book with an understanding of the range of possibilities, and the necessary steps involved in conceiving, planning and implementing your marketing. That's not an easy thing to find!

Not easy to find? Why is that?

A major reason is that most of the online marketing specialists who you could study with make their living by specializing, not by giving you the big picture. For instance, you'll find many choices of teachers and programs when it comes to learning about Facebook advertising, building an email list, optimizing your Linked In profile, deciding on your company name, choosing your Ideal Client, enrolling new clients, and so much more.

What you WON'T find are many teachers who will help you see the view from 10,000 feet, to understand the big overall picture of marketing – and then also drill down to the nitty gritty with you. To a large extent, we've done that for you here, and our book stands out for that reason.

Another reason it can be challenging to find a marketing coach or mentor that's perfect for YOU is that many business coaches and mentors lack experience in running solo businesses. They've cut their teeth on larger enterprises, or even in corporate America, and thus, their perspective, while sometimes useful, often is not relevant enough and can even be discouraging. To learn more about the role of the marketing coach, see Step 8: ENLIST.

About the depth and breadth of what you'll find here...

There has been a continual give and take between that 10,000-foot view I mentioned and the desire to give you useful how-to information. The result is that we've gone into considerable depth in a few areas and moderate depth in others. In every case, the information we've provided (such as that in Step 6: SELECT and Step 7: BUILD), will be practical and helpful in nature. We're committed to giving you a thorough overview, and also to helping you understand how to make the decisions that you'll be facing.

One thing our book doesn't do is go into great depth about marketing on the internet.

Internet marketing is a vast topic and a technical topic. In order to succeed, your best practices must change quickly and frequently in response to changes in such unknowable things as Google and Facebook policies and algorithms. For many of you, especially if you're planning to build a local business, a broad understanding of the intricacies of internet marketing won't be necessary for you to succeed. For others, it will be a necessity. We have included several sections of introductory information on internet marketing practices to help you get started in the chapters on Steps 6: SELECT and 7: BUILD. We've also broken down some of the terms that often confuse and stop people from getting started on the internet, and shared advice on how to choose a service to build a website.

By way of follow-up after you've completed our book:

We've included a resources section, entitled *Ways and Means,* which will lead you to additional sources of information.

Finally, we've briefly outlined the 20 different coaching programs we have available to help you implement what you've learned here if you desire hands-on assistance in one or more areas. See *How We Can Help: Life Force Marketing Services* chapter at the end of the book.

Okay! Time to get started! We hope you enjoy, and are inspired by, every word. ☺

Is Our Book for You?

"The world's largest workforce works for itself."

I've heard that recently in online commercials for Quicken accounting services. It has a tantalizing ring to it. Another way to say this is -- most people are self-employed! That's a pretty startling statement. I'm curious, and perhaps you are too: How much of this work force is comprised of one- or two-person businesses?

You may be surprised to learn (as I was) that the Small Business Association's official definition of a 'small business' is "any company with fewer than 500 employees." I don't know about you, but that doesn't seem very small to me!

There's also another business classification known as "micro-business." These companies have 5 or fewer employees, and they represent 92% of all U.S. businesses! *(According to an Association for Enterprise Opportunity report)* Perhaps that's the "world's largest workforce" Quicken was talking about in their commercial – at least in the U.S.A.

I designed Life Force Marketing with the particular perspective of the micro-business in mind. It's intended to serve solopreneurs and tiny enterprises of five or fewer people.

To further clarify, this book puts its emphasis on solo service providers who are in the holistic healing or creative fields, those I'd describe as "mission-driven service providers."

Life Force Marketing is for practitioners with a strong sense of purpose.

Because holistic marketing has, at its core, a strong sense of purpose, it will not feel comfortable or relevant to business people who operate strictly to make money. It will, on the other hand, seem relevant to those of us who are on a mission, who feel called to contribute to the world.

This book is for people who want to have lucrative businesses and private practices, but who also have a larger purpose beyond the financial motivators.

This tribe includes but is certainly not limited to such professionals as:

- massage therapists and cranio-sacral therapists
- Feldenkrais, Alexander and Trager practitioners
- health and wellness coaches, consultants and advisors
- occupational and physical therapists
- holistic voice, theater, dance and visual art coaches
- breath workers, energy workers, and intuitive healers
- Feng Shui practitioners and Ikebana masters
- naturopaths, homeopaths, and acupuncturists
- sexual empowerment advisers
- personal trainers
- spiritual and life coaches and career counselors
- dance, art and music therapists
- yoga and Pilates teachers

It is also for people in transition, those who have spent a lifetime working for someone else and may want to try their hands at self-employment by serving others in some way. Making this kind of leap, from being an employee to being self-employed, is challenging. At Life Force Marketing we know how to help with your decision-making process and also with the implementation stages.

Regardless of exactly what your profession is, this book is meant to guide you through ten steps that can transform your understanding of how to promote yourself and your services to others so you can live the Life you're envisioning for yourself.

I wonder, do you feel at home here?

What is Holistic Marketing?

Holism is the idea that systems* are integrated wholes, not just a collection of parts. Holistic principles apply in many fields: education, somatic studies, medicine, religion, anthropology, environmental studies, nursing, and more.

(Holism applies to physical, biological, chemical, social, economic, mental, and linguistic systems, too. *Thanks Wikipedia!*)

The essence of holism is that something occurring in one part of a system will affect other parts.

I use the word 'holistic' in this context because, in the Life Force approach to marketing, I advocate that when making your decisions and developing your strategies, you take into account many inter-dependent factors:

- The kind of work that's deeply important to you
- Your prosperity mindset
- Your currently available resources (a new way of looking at your assets)
- Your understanding of the clients you want to attract and serve, and the problems you can help solve on their behalf
- The inspiration and results you plan to provide your clientele
- The relationship between your marketing strategies and your financial goals
- How your marketing activities can provide something your clients will find valuable, even before they buy from you
- Your way of locating, interviewing, staying in touch with, and retaining clients
- The alignment of marketing strategies with your values, ethical standards, strengths, interests and financial goals
- The impact your marketing efforts can have on your belief in yourself and your engagement in your community

All of this is interconnected. If your Vision isn't clear, your message won't be either. If you're still telling yourself old undermining stories about yourself, no website or social media campaign will get you what you want. If you aren't operating within your ethical guidelines, you can't possibly speak authentically and persuasively about your work. If you aren't making enough money, your self-confidence will suffer. If you don't feel connected to your community, you'll feel a disconnect when promoting your services.

You can attract clients the same way you heal clients, holistically.

Traditional marketing, much like Western medicine, is often invasive. Too often, marketing is ruthless, manipulative and neglectful of the needs of everyone except the seller. On the other hand, holistic marketing, like holistic healing, is noninvasive and mindful of all interconnected factors.

As a practitioner, holistic marketing is designed to increase your prosperity without compromising your values and to provide meaningful, trustworthy connections between you and the people who are desperately trying to find you.

Holistic marketing leads to a win-win professional lifestyle where both the buyer and the seller get what they were looking for, and the process of getting there is educational, enjoyable and uplifting.

As a mission-driven service provider, you can feel comfortable taking the path of holistic marketing. It's designed to balance the needs of prospective clients and your professional desires. By practicing this approach, you'll begin to recognize how your marketing itself provides a service to others, within an ethical framework that feels valuable to all concerned. Because of the win-win situations you've created, you'll be able to take care of your marketing duties without dread, embarrassment or apology.

With a holistic foundation for your marketing efforts, you can do good things for your pocketbook. You can move in the direction of your larger mission. And you can remain true to your values. You will increase the amount of good you do in the world.

Note: The term 'holistic marketing' is not always defined in precisely the way it's used in *Life Force Marketing*. In order to express my marketing ideology; I've made an expanded definition of holistic marketing, which has some similarities to -- but is also different in some regards -- from the standard definition.

Tips for using our book

- There's value in just reading this book, but you will receive so much more if you work with some of the many suggested action steps. Taking action is what will move you forward. You may wish to read it once without doing the action steps, and then go through a second time in more detail, focusing on the sections you found most helpful and relevant to your circumstances.

- Designate a notebook, journal, or online file folder just for this work. As you're working your way through, you'll generate good ideas. Having all your thoughts in one place will be helpful. Because there's a generous amount of white space in our book, you could also write in the margins.

- I've organized our book so that what you do, think about, and learn in each chapter builds to the next. There's a definite advantage in going from beginning to end.

- To solve the problem of pronouns, you'll notice I often switch between masculine and feminine, singular and plural.

- Take advantage of the *Here's Something You Can Do Right Now* sections. They'll lead you to the heart of the matter.

- Stay in touch! Share your questions, ideas and breathtaking realizations by contacting us at www.LifeForceMarketing.com/CONTACT

Legend

Many additional resources are waiting for you on our website. This symbol indicates you can find more information on a particular subject at: **www.LifeForceMarketing.com/MORE**

This symbol means: **"This is something we at Life Force Marketing can help you with."** Not sure if you need our help? You're welcome to request a conversation to help you determine your next steps. Request a Complimentary Consultation from our website Contact Us page:

www.LifeForceMarketing.com/CONTACT

Periodically you'll see a reminder: *"Take a Moment … Breathe."* I've placed these symbols at points in our book where it may be a good idea to pause and let everything sink in. You might stand up, walk around, drink water, get some fresh air, play with your cat or dog, take a shower, do a jig -- allow what you've just read to incubate before continuing.

Why pause?

* Describing what is now known as the incubation effect, (respected psychoanalyst Rollo May) notes from anecdotal experience that the unconscious mind...(finds) insight only if the conscious mind has first struggled to find a solution... (Later), when the conscious mind gives up and transitions into a state of relaxation, the unconscious mind often completes the job, and we exhale "Aha!"

* "Rollo May and the Courage to Create," by Joachim Krueger Ph.D., posted online in Psychology Today, February 16, 2016.

Perhaps a little break from reading will lead to your "AHA!"

About the ART Work

Some years ago, I read a book entitled *Succulent Wild Woman*, written by a creative fireball of a writer and teacher named SARK. I love her book, in part because it's full of color and little drawings that delight the reader and keep us reading and musing.

From the first moments of planning this book, I knew it would be colorful and art-filled.

I think of the cartoons, drawings, abstract paintings and computer-enhanced pieces you'll find intertwined here with the text as providing a respite from thinking, a visual incentive to pause and drink in the colors and shapes or get a giggle from the cartoons. With the abstracts, in particular, I hope you'll treat them like you might the clouds in the sky, asking "What do I see here?" Usually, they relate in some way to the topic at hand.

I hope you enjoy the visual elements of our book as much as I enjoyed SARKS'!

All of the artwork in this book was drawn, painted, photographed or 'collaged' either by myself or someone who attended one of our group art-making parties.

Many of these images are available as greeting cards on my website: GoodTidingsCards.com

Thanks go to those who have participated in Good Tidings art-making: Angela Rae, Balin Kruse-Williams, Carole Kruse, Carolyne Slayton-Knox, Debbie Stoops, Elizabeth Schafer Humphrey, Gene Williams, Maria Paglialungo, Matthew Schuler, Melissa Amarral, Melody Cooper, Miki Wright, Oyo Fumilayo, Roshan Nikou, Samantha Moore, Sonja Davis, Susan Smith-Sargent, Susan Stern, and Vera Thomas, to name a few. We've had a lot of fun together.

Additional thanks go to Duncan Veach from Lexington, Kentucky's premier printing company for visual artists: Beau Graphics. Because of Beau Graphics, I have a reliable local option for printing my greeting cards and everything else.

part one

Igniting the Fires of Intention

Great accomplishments begin by declaring
clear intentions, believing in the
possibility of their attainment,
and gathering every
available resource
to bring them to Life.

Envision

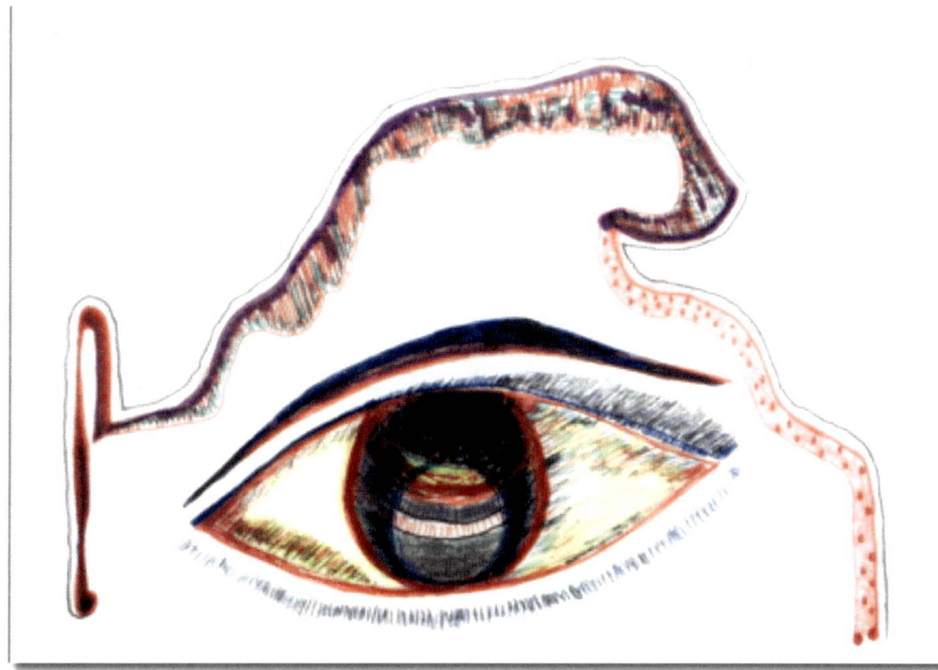

When you are inspired by some great purpose, some extraordinary project, all your thoughts break their bonds: Your mind transcends limitations, your consciousness expands in every direction, and you find yourself in a new, great and wonderful world. Dormant forces, faculties and talents become alive, and you discover yourself to be a greater person by far than you ever dreamed yourself to be.

Patanjali

Envision

Step One
Envision the Life You'd Love to Live

We start our process with Envisioning because, without a Vision, you're like a ship without a destination. If your understanding of what you want to accomplish is vague, if for some reason you haven't expended the time and energy needed to define your intentions clearly, you'll be shortchanging your prosperity efforts.

It's a fairly well-kept secret that having a splendid, technicolor, 'felt' Vision for yourself that thrills you to the very marrow of your bones is what provides the Life Force required for building and growing an enterprise and living a prosperous Life.

We begin, at Step One, with fleshing out a Vision for what you want to accomplish, the type of practice or business you want to build, the people you want to serve, what you want to offer them, the results you want to facilitate for them, the environment in which you'll do this, and everything else that defines prosperity for you.

This process, and those suggested in steps two and three will help you begin to communicate the clearest possible intentions to every person you encounter who's interested in collaborating with you, hiring you, writing about you, or recommending you to someone else.

You need a vision so exciting that it pulls you out of bed in the morning. Building a business is hard work and it may require actions that stretch you out of your comfort zone. You may have to put in more hours of effort than you are accustomed to, especially in the beginning. Avoiding the extra work may be appealing at times!

Being able to feel and taste what it will be like once you have achieved your Vision will give you the will to overcome obstacles or difficulties that arise. Your 'felt' Vision will give you the motivation to do what's needed. Ideally, your Vision will become so real to you that it will make you want to do the work required to achieve it. If you don't have a strong Vision to lean on, it will be easier to give up on your dreams and settle for less.

As will be made clear as you read along, your Vision for the Life you want to live and the broader mission you have for your work will also inform every marketing decision you make.

Moving forward without a vivid, heartfelt Vision
may be a form of planning to fail.

Without it, you lack the fuel needed to project a powerful, clear intention and keep your warrior spirit alive as you craft your Life-altering business from the ethers. And that's why holistic marketing must begin with the development of a Vision that will guide and motivate you every step along the way to building your ideal practice or business.

REVELATIONS: Thinking freely, imagining boundlessly

When I was 25 years old, I attended my first network marketing presentation. I had been invited to a friend's house in Berkeley, California to learn about a new business idea. I was, even then, sprouting entrepreneurial wings (although I didn't know it yet). By far the most memorable moment of that evening was when someone flipped over a piece of large white paper he had suspended on an easel and asked a very provocative question, "If money was no object, what would you do, where would you go, and what would you have?" This was an Earth-shaking event for me at the time for the simple reason that no-one had ever suggested that I think so freely, imagine so boundlessly. Undoubtedly that's why I still remember it clearly today.

I've since heard many variations on this kind of question, each designed to stimulate thinking beyond the current personal paradigm. One of my favorites is the oft-quoted, "What would you do if you knew you couldn't fail?" This question stirs me deeply; I use it often to motivate myself when I notice that I'm dragging my feet, or my confidence is waning. This brilliant question goes to the core of what stops many of us from reaching for the stars — our fear that we will fail.

More recently I've learned a paradigm-busting question that's fool-proof for stimulating a grand Life Vision. From Mary Morrissey, the creator of Dreambuilder Coaching, this potent question is, "What is the Life you would love to live?" I suggest you begin here:

What is the Life you would love to live?

Why is Envisioning Something We Postpone?

In the past ten years, I've attended many online courses, seminars, live events and symposia on topics related to growing a small business or private practice. In most of those events, there's been some mention of Envisioning. Predictably, most people in the field of business coaching and mentoring agree that having a Vision is essential. Some refer to your Vision as "Your Why." Despite the almost universal agreement, I've noticed something ironic. Although each of these talented teachers, leaders, and speakers has a highly developed and detailed curriculum, only a few give any serious attention to the Envisioning segments of their programs! I often wonder if there's an assumption operating, something like, "This Vision-Building stuff is something anyone can do, so let's just get it over with and jump into the hard stuff!"

This is an erroneous assumption because, sadly, for many people, Envisioning is difficult. When we're trying to create a Vision of our possible future and sustain that Vision over time while the new circumstances unfold, it's all the more challenging. I've witnessed first-hand as talented aspirational people comment about how hard it is to imagine a boundless future, and I've experienced it myself.

As the influential author Wallace Wattles, wrote, "There is no labor from which most people shrink as they do from that of sustained and consecutive thought; it is the hardest work in the world." This tendency applies to sustained and consecutive thought about a personal and professional Vision.

I've heard many reasons to explain this reluctance to spend time on Envisioning. Some people say they feel stuck in an old view of themselves and can't see anything grander or more satisfying in the future. Others contend that Envisioning reinforces a long-held belief that they're not creative and don't have much imagination. Still others express that Envisioning something far outside of their current circumstances seems like wishful thinking. Some are vaguely uncomfortable imagining their future but don't know why.

Our efforts to envision a prosperous Life thrive on our self-confidence.

A firm belief in one's self makes us more willing to try, willing to risk, willing to explore, and more able to attract our Good.

Because I understand that Envisioning is both profoundly necessary and, yet, often confusing or frustrating, I emphasize it in my one-to-one coaching. We're going to go into it more deeply here as well.

Becoming a more agile imaginer is possible.

The imagination is much like a muscle -- it benefits from frequent use.

If you do two dozen biceps curls with weights, three times a week, your biceps will get stronger. You can count on that. The same goes for training your imaginative functions. You become stronger and more agile with practice.

I've put together *6 Actions to Ignite Your Powerful Vision*, an Envisioning process that can help you create your very own technicolor inspiring vision of the practice/business you want to build.

---

6 ACTIONS TO IGNITE YOUR POWERFUL VISION

1
Ask Provocative Questions

2
Exercise Your Imagination by Thinking Bigger

3
Document Your Vision

4
Share Your Vision with Someone Else

5
Imagine Your Success and Feel the Excitement

6
Treat Your Vision as a Living Breathing Thing

1
Ignite Your Powerful Vision
Ask Provocative Questions

Asking questions is something I've done for a living for over 18 years as a Feldenkrais Practitioner. I've learned that asking and answering thought-provoking questions can direct awareness and thinking to surprising new places. Asking provocative questions shines a light on the details of Life and often leads to deeper revelation.

A few examples of provocative questions:

First, I suggest you try mining the past in a *general* way:

- What's one thing you love doing but haven't done in a very long time?
- Is there something you've always wanted to do but can't seem to prioritize?
- Is there a particular kind of lifestyle that, when you see others enjoying it, you feel a longing to Do, Be or Have something similar?
- Is there something that you used to believe you could Do, Be or Have but, somewhere along the line, you gave up on it?

Second, ask a few questions specifically related to building a more substantial business:

- Who are the people you'd most enjoy having as clients? How many clients would you love to have? How many months of the year would you like to work?
- If you could be known as an expert in solving a particular problem, what would it be?
- What would your clients say or write about you and your work? Your colleagues and peers?
- Where would you love to practice, in what sort of environment? Locally or remotely?
- How much money would you love to be making? What would you be able to do with the money you'd be making? If you had a magic wand, what would you create?

2

Ignite Your Powerful Vision

Exercise Your Imagination by Thinking Bigger

When you first try Envisioning the Life and the practice you want, unless you're quite used to exercising your imagination in this way, you may find your ideas a little bit on the dull side, or slow in coming. Likewise, if you see that what you're imagining seems "okay" but falls short in the thrill factor, you may be thinking too small.

Rather than exercising your imagination, you're probably exercising too much caution!

Try making your vision BIGGER! Reach for something outrageous! As best-selling author and coach Brendon Burchard often teaches, "Raise Your Ambitions!"

When you're building your Vision, that's not the time to think incrementally! The step-by-step part comes later. Do not limit your Vision to something you already know how to do. Now is the time to think big enough that when you put yourself in the picture, it feels like you've "tapped into something magical." (Thank you Ryan Eliason)

The reason that a worthy Vision sends a shiver through your entire Self is: That's your Life Force speaking!

REVELATIONS: Dance bigger, think bigger

I have to confess that, for many years as a younger woman, I resisted the idea of thinking bigger. Because I was already struggling to get by, *thinking bigger* seemed out of the question. One of the first people to challenge my point of view directly was a business partner I had while working with Amway Corporation in the San Francisco Bay area. His name was Orrin Wright.

Orrin was a statuesque, effervescent, drop-dead gorgeous professional ballroom dancer with a mesmerizing personality. I was an intermediate student of African and Modern dance who had just moved to California from rural Kentucky. Orrin, who I regarded as a rock star, saw more in me than I saw in myself.

Often, he and his life partner would host elaborate parties at their lavish San Francisco home and invite all their business partners. On these occasions, at some point, everyone in the spacious ballroom would move away from the center and make room for Orrin to dance. Inevitably he would come and extend his hand and invite me to be his partner. I had no training or experience in ballroom dance whatsoever, but because Orrin saw a grand vision for the two of us as dance partners (and because he had a very strong lead!), each time

I managed to stay with him as we practically flew through the room, turning, dipping and gliding to the music and applause. This experience was both ecstatic and terrifying for me. There's little doubt that because Orrin insisted on thinking bigger for me, I began to think bigger, too.

Over time I've found that Orrin, Brendon, and Ryan are right. When we maintain an open invitation to think bigger, we can pop the lid off of something! We can reach a turning point. By stretching your ability to dream, you will find your way out of habitual thinking, and into an enhanced view of your True Calling. We can imagine bigger goals that are worthier of the time, energy, commitment, and work it will take to achieve them. Let's return to the classic, provocative question I mentioned earlier. You can use it to stimulate bigger thinking.

What would you do if you knew you couldn't fail?

Ask yourself that question and look out! A torrent of ideas will soon start coming your way. Try not to be afraid of your biggest ideas. Trust yourself! After all, your desires may be the most unambiguous clues you have about the best next direction for your Life.

You can fail at what you don't want, so you might as well take a chance at doing what you love.

Jim Carrey

3
Ignite Your Powerful Vision
Document Your Vision

It's imperative to take your growing Vision out of your mental lockbox and put it in some other form where you can observe and interact with it. Documenting your Vision makes it more concrete, and thus more possible. There are many ways to do this:

1. Write down the answers to your provocative questions on big paper with crayons or marker pens and tape it to your wall!

2. Do a 'Before and After' of some kind: represent how things are for you now, and then represent how they might look when you've moved substantially toward your Vision. You can do this through drawing or painting, making a collage or voice recording.

3. Write a song or letter to a friend sharing your Vision.

4. Finally, perhaps the best-known means of documenting your Vision: Make a vision board.

Note: Finding the perfect photos to represent a Vision has become much simpler with the advent of the internet. You no longer have to go sifting through piles of magazines (unless you happen to enjoy that). You can find a picture of anything online and print it out on your home printer.

5. Choose the style of documenting that feels accessible to you, the one that you would enjoy doing most. On the other hand, don't be afraid to try something new! That in itself will stimulate your imagination.

By documenting your Vision, you're creating the daily ammunition you need to keep it alive in your conscious mind, top of mind. See tips for making a Vision Board on our site. LifeForceMarketing.com/MORE

We remember things better when they're attached to a picture. 65% better to be exact.... A picture can create movements. A picture can unite nations. A picture can pull at your heart and fill you with a deep desire to do something... You don't have to be an artist or know how to draw. When you draw where you are -- your current state -- and where you want to be -- your desired new reality -- suddenly you have a roadmap for change.

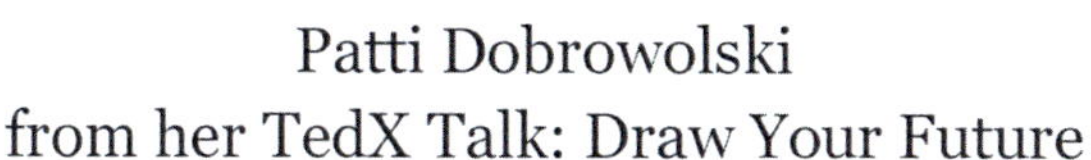
Patti Dobrowolski
from her TedX Talk: Draw Your Future

4

Ignite Your Powerful Vision

Share Your Vision with Someone Else

Strap on your seatbelt! We're moving into a transformative exercise.

I realize that you may have some resistance to sharing your Vision with someone else (out loud, no less!) Sharing your Vision with another may be uncomfortable, but if you push through the discomfort, you'll be pressing into your growing edge.

Perhaps you feel like your Vision is just a bunch of crazy impossible wishful thinking. If that's the case, you might feel embarrassed to tell someone else about your true desires, what you truly want.

I understand. Let's be real here! Sharing a big Vision for your future, especially if what you're longing for is something different than the Life you're living today, can feel like sticking your neck out. Many people feel shy about doing this.

I have a few suggestions to help you get started.

First, have a little chat with yourself.

Make a determined statement to yourself that your Vision is valid whether or not anyone else agrees with it. Come to think of it, why would you expect someone else to understand your desires totally? After all, 'someone else' isn't inside your head, inside your heart. They're not living YOUR life! Own your Vision, and you'll feel a lot less shy about sharing it!

Choose wisely.

Think about who your allies are in Life.

Who in your Life is capable of listening to you in a receptive way? Who, if you asked them to do so, would allow you to share something that's important to you and agree in advance not to judge what they've heard? That's the person to choose.

Maybe it's a dear close friend. Maybe it's your sister or brother, or a friend who's always supported you. If you're lucky, it may be your spouse or your child! Whoever it is, find someone you can talk to who will agree in advance to be a receptive listener and to avoid criticizing what you say.

Employ your pet!

If you are truly terrified to do this, describe your Vision to your pet first so that you can get used to saying and hearing it aloud! (No, I'm not kidding…) Describe your Vision for your Life, your business or practice in detail to your dog, your parrot, your cat, your horse, or your flying squirrel! Soon you'll be ready to share it with a person. At the very least you'll become accustomed to hearing it out aloud.

Final thoughts on speaking your Vision aloud.

The actual acts of visualizing, then writing about, and finally verbalizing what you've imagined have differing physiological effects. Each of these actions activates a different sector of your brain. So, when you talk about your Vision, something happens in your brain that doesn't if you merely write about it.

(*L.A.Times.com*, "Writing and speaking come from different parts of the brain, study shows" by Carolyn Kellogg. May 13, 2015)

From both a marketing and educational standpoint, exercising your 'speaking brain system' is a good idea, and will help you become more expert in communicating about your practice and services.

5

Ignite Your Powerful Vision

Imagine Your Success and Feel the Excitement

As you contemplate your mission and what you would love for your private practice or business, look for the imaginary ideas that cause you to light up, that are thrilling to you in body, mind and, spirit. Allow yourself to get excited about it!

Your Vision has the capacity to propel you forward; however, in order for that effect to be ignited, you will need the potency that comes from "feeling the future."

Feeling your Vision is, in many ways, the most influential part and, yet, the most elusive part of the Envisioning process. To feel excited about something that hasn't happened yet requires a no-holds-barred commitment to believing that the realization of your Vision is a possibility rather than a pipe dream.

I was referring to this tricky practice earlier when I wrote about "keeping the warrior spirit alive as you craft your life-altering business from the ethers." If you can continue to envision what you want and to feel what it will be like when it comes to pass, you'll be on the road to fulfilling your intention. We'll talk more about this in Step 2: REVISE.

6

Ignite Your Powerful Vision

Treat Your Vision as a Living, Breathing Thing

Even though you're documenting your Vision, that doesn't mean it's going to remain static and never change. On the contrary, the best idea is to visit your Vision every day and revise it monthly. Think of it as a living, breathing thing that needs your attention to survive, grow and evolve. Use your documentation – your writing, or drawings, voice recording, video or vision board -- as something to interact with so you can review it and revise it on a regular basis. That's a commitment worth making.

Alert! Important heads up!

There will absolutely be days when some old ways of thinking will try to weigh you down and keep you from believing in your Vision. Expect this to happen so you won't be surprised when it does! We'll address this at length in Step 2: REVISE.

Nonetheless, even in the presence of doubt or diminishing belief in your Vision -- in fact, as an antidote to that doubt -- commit to interacting with your Vision in some form every single day, even if it's just for one minute. Don't let an old style of thinking keep you from connecting with what you really want and owning it.

If you'll take these six simple actions to heart and turn them into a Life practice, you'll notice a new clarity arising.

As you work with it, your Vision will become more real to you! You'll start to see ways in which you can clarify and tweak it to more accurately reflect what you desire.

In turn, by visiting your Vision daily and doing the necessary actions, your desire will become clearer and more defined.

You'll also begin to see how you can move in the direction of what you want. Your intuition will kick in. Good ideas will start floating to the surface.

You'll notice that, as your Vision becomes more real to you, you'll also feel happy more often and unexpectedly. Having a Vision provides you with intrinsic motivation.

Envisioning is the ultimate prosperity practice.

I'd like to share a final bit of guidance…

If you find that you're not able to imagine very freely just yet, try not to be hard on yourself or become discouraged!

Because your imagination is like a muscle, the more you use it, the more toned it becomes. You simply need to practice, so try again tomorrow.

I've added several Imagination Exercises on my website for your experimentation. They're short and fun to do. You might sense immediate results! You can become adept at imagining, even if you don't currently view yourself as a creative person. LifeForceMarketing.com/MORE

Here's something you can do right now.

- Take a moment to quiet your mind.
- Take one of the provocative questions from the beginning of this chapter and begin to write down your answers or speak them into the voice recorder on your smartphone.
- Open up to your imagination and permit yourself to think freely, without judgment.
- Be honest with yourself about what you desire.
- Set aside some time for this, at least 20 minutes, maybe an hour. Once your imagination gets warmed up, more ideas will start to flow.
- You'll revisit this often, but start with what you can imagine right here, right now.
- Remember: You don't need any magical qualities, to be a creative genius, nor do you need special DNA. Whether you know it or not, being creative is your birthright. Your imagination is your gateway to the creative impulse you came into this world with at birth.
- Celebrate every victory! Celebrate making headway with your Vision. Celebrate loving yourself so much you're able to be honest about your desires.

"Feed your faith and your doubts will starve to death..."

wisdom from the World Wide Web

Revise

As the observer of the contents of my mind,
I must be more than the contents of my mind.

Cardell and Linn Vermilion Smith
Quantum Life Changes

Step Two
Revise the Story You Tell Yourself About Yourself

This chapter is about something often referred to in Prosperity Studies as 'Belief Work.' In it, we'll talk about the stories we tell ourselves and the personal deeply held beliefs behind those stories – all part of the incessant mental chatter we live with every day. We'll learn:

- How these beliefs and stories affect your progress toward new achievements
- Where the stories come from, and how your point of view alters your interpretation of them
- A practice for disempowering these stories right on the spot, to gradually revise your beliefs and stories and replace them with something more in line with your Vision.

Revising is step two in the Life Force Marketing process because, any time you entertain a larger Vision, you can expect to experience a backlash. Envisioning a Life more abundant, freer, more satisfying than the one you are currently living automatically stimulates the appearance of entrenched oppositional beliefs.

When you're on the road to marketing yourself and your services to create a more prosperous Life, it's almost a certainty that you'll be accosted on multiple occasions by nagging, inaccurate, undermining beliefs and their accompanying mood shifts. These occurrences can have a seductive negative influence on your ability to keep making progress -- unless you learn to recognize what's happening and have a practice in place for minimizing their impact. Let's get started.

How Your Beliefs and Stories Affect You

The Life you currently live has gathered a lot of momentum. You, and also the people in your Life, tend to believe in your apparent current limitations mainly because there's so much proof they are real.

Often when we try to envision something new, such as a more purpose-filled, prosperous Life, the judgmental and 'practical' voices that reinforce our current limitations try to slow us down. That's why Envisioning an expanded, more satisfying Life requires continual, repeated engagement.

As you know, our minds are continually cranking out thoughts. Most of the time we barely even notice the content of these thoughts in any real detail. They pass across the movie screen of our lives, mostly unexamined. From time to time, however, some of this mental activity becomes louder and more insistent. Our thoughts call in additional similar ones and, BINGO! We begin to feel an emotion. We get upset, feel jealous, start crying, feel a surge of joy, get angry, or become mildly depressed – all in an instant.

When this happens, maybe it's because one of our passing thoughts has stimulated an emotional reaction. Some would say it's the other way around, the emotions come first, triggering thoughts. Who knows? Is it the chicken or the egg? Does it matter? If we see the body and mind as inseparable, the significance is more theoretical than practical.

The point is, often our undermining beliefs and accompanying emotional reactions take center stage at the most inconvenient times.

> "A belief is only a thought I keep thinking."
>
> Abraham Hicks

How do your undermining thoughts sound to you?

The late Ken Keyes, Jr., Founder of the Living Love Method and author of the best seller: *Handbook to Higher Consciousness,* called our unconscious beliefs "core beliefs." You may recognize one or two of them!

- I can't do it.
- I can't have what I want.
- I don't deserve happiness.
- I fail no matter how hard I try.
- I have to suffer in some way to receive prosperity.
- I'm not respected.
- Life is full of stress and overload.
- The world is an unhappy place.

Visit our site for a lengthier list of core beliefs and also the Twelve Pathways of Ken Keyes' Living Love Method. It's potent stuff! LifeForceMarketing.com/MORE

What is the difference between beliefs and stories?

For this discussion, we'll use the term 'beliefs' to describe the subterranean, often unconscious conclusions we've come to about ourselves and about Life. These conclusions are often hard to pin down because we rarely look at them directly. They influence us, but not usually in a conscious way.

'Stories,' as we use the word in Belief work, refers to the narratives we construct about ourselves to make sense of all these beliefs and to put them in a broader context.

To illustrate, I'll share a personal story I used to tell myself (unconsciously) about myself. *Ouch.* I sometimes wonder how I survived my own thinking.

"I'm a small-town Kentucky girl, raised in a divorced family and an oppressive cultural environment in which girls aren't highly valued. I didn't receive an adequate education and I was too busy with my social life to buckle down and study, so I didn't do as well as I could have. Partly because of that, I have a hard time being around people who are more educated and worldly than myself."

There were deep-seated beliefs at work here, which could be stated as follows:

- Sophisticated, well-educated people don't value small town girls from Kentucky.
- I'm under-educated and inferior to those with more education or who have seen more of the world than I.
- I am lazy and don't do the work needed to excel.
- Because of the way some people treated me as a young girl, I didn't have high self-esteem as a young woman, and thus I'm not as successful as I should be.

See how the beliefs and the story go hand in hand? The unconscious beliefs are buried, not easy to see. The way to find them is to listen to the story you're telling yourself. That's not easy either! Still, if you're quiet, you'll hear it running underneath the surface, steadily broadcasting the same nonsense, over and over.

Not all beliefs are negative.

Not at all! You probably hold many positive beliefs about yourself and those are influential, too! If you have grown up in a healthy, happy home and supportive community environment, and if you've been spared horrendous trauma or loss -- you probably have many positive beliefs about yourself. Thus, you'll undoubtedly tell yourself much more positive stories than you might, for instance, if you grew up in a dysfunctional home with absentee parents and constant financial struggle, in a neighborhood with a drug dealer on every corner.

I'm not trying to be political here; it's just common sense. I'm also not trying to say that human behavior is all about environmental influences; heredity has its say in the matter, too.

The good news is that no matter what system of beliefs you've built up so far, or the source of those beliefs, you can alter many of them through practice. Your ability to do so is something we'll discuss later in the chapter.

How do you know when you're bumping into one of your limiting belief systems?

You may sense the presence of your 'judging mind,' branding your ideas as far-fetched, impractical, naive or downright impossible.

You may notice pessimistic mental chatter or unexplained boredom. Your mind might nag you with repetitive, critical thoughts. You may feel discouraged or ashamed for no apparent reason.

Sometimes the symptom will be a general sense of confusion or purposelessness, an unexplained lack of focus.

Quite likely, when this occurs, you'll be tempted to stop believing in your Vision. You may hear a voice say, "I can't make this happen." or "Who do you think you are?" or "Every time you try something like this, you fail."

With a little practice, you'll begin to recognize when this is happening in real time!

Ironically, once you've embarked on an Envisioning process and have something bigger and better to reach for, the appearance of such voices and feelings is a sure sign you're on the right track! You're upsetting the part of yourself that works diligently to maintain your status quo and keep you in familiar territory. If you hear these voices, you've stirred something up, and that's progress in itself.

Where Your Stories Come From and How You Interpret Them

Throughout your Lifetime you've painstakingly built up a story you tell yourself about yourself. Much of this story is either false or severely outdated.

This story is predicated on beliefs you've acquired about Life, yourself and the people around you. As we've said, these beliefs, collectively, make up your personal story.

Most of us have perpetually and quietly repeated some form of our personal stories again, and again, tens of thousands of times. Partly due to all this repetition, they seem believable. We may go for years at a time without questioning whether or not they're true.

Each time you take action or think of taking action, each time you try and fail or try and succeed, each circumstance you hope for and have ever hoped for, each thing that always makes you laugh or cry, the highly personal ways you deal with authority figures and the unknown, how you react to surprises or deadlines, the circumstances in which you feel triumphant and in which you feel humiliated, the kind of activities you do and do not participate in, the style of clothes you do and do not wear, the money you do and do not make – even the way you pick up your coffee cup — all of this and much more goes into molding an inner impression you have of yourself, forming your beliefs, and composing your story.

Add to this the accidents you've had, the pregnancies you've lived through, the actions you've taken with your right hand but not your left, the sports you've been a part of, the instruments you've played, the dances you've practiced, the periods when you were sedentary, the time spent in a cast or hospital bed, the years you spent carrying children, singing in a jazz band, pressing into your clients' deep tissue or leaning into a computer screen — this too has contributed to the inner impressions you carry of yourself and, thus, your beliefs. Finally, mix in the times you've been in love, had fun, been betrayed, hated someone or were hated, forgave or refused to forgive, were insulted or praised, undermined or exalted and all the rest...

This inner personal impression is more than a mental construct; it's a 'felt sense' of who you are at the core. Your felt sense of self, containing all the millions of impressions you've received about yourself over a lifetime, has unconsciously formed your beliefs about yourself and thus your personal story.

Your beliefs and your story live somewhere in your mind and in the hidden crevices of your body – in your bodymind -- and they influence every action you take *and don't take.*

Another way to say this is that, over time, you've adopted the view that you're THIS kind of person, but not THAT kind of person. Consequently, you've become less and less likely to do anything that disagrees with your current story. As evidence of the power of this phenomenon, consider this thought-provoking quote from a TEDX talk called *Draw Your Future.*

> "Research shows the odds against you making a change in your life are 9 to 1. Even if you're facing a life-threatening illness."
>
> Patti Dobrowolski

That's a sobering thought, right? I appreciate this research because it reminds me of what we're up against!

Gradually, without really noticing, you've concluded that this personal inner impression, this view of yourself, acquired over time, is who you are.

It is not.

Your inner self-impression and felt sense of self, your beliefs and the stories you tell yourself are derived from your current and historical thinking, feeling, moving and sensing. This composite of identity elements is what Dr. Moshe Feldenkrais, physicist and developer of the Feldenkrais Method of Movement Education®, called your "self-image."

Another way to understand self-image is to think of it as an embodied anchor for the stories you tell yourself about yourself. Your self-image helps to keep your old paradigm, your habitual way of thinking about yourself, securely in place.

Allow me to clarify: It's not that there's no truth at all in your time-honored stories. It's merely that these narratives only tell a small part of the story of who you are -- and for this book -- who you can become, who you need to become to build a more prosperous business than you've had in the past.

> "We are veritable walking libraries filled with stories about ourselves, our lives, the way things work, who we should work with, the value of our modality, how much money we can earn, what we want and what's an acceptable way to get it."
>
> Allison Rapp, Feldenkrais Trainer and
> Transformational Practice-Building Coach

To have more freedom to move around in the world, to be less tethered to beliefs and stories that are, at best, incomplete renderings of who you are — it seems essential to question in some detail whether the stories are legitimate.

To learn more about the Feldenkrais Method of Movement Education, and other methods for altering the story you tell yourself about yourself, visit our book's *Addendum*.

Please note that your stories aren't necessarily built on facts! Rather, many of them derive from your interpretation of events at the time they occurred and your memory of them long after the fact.

Better say that again!

The stories you tell about yourself to yourself and others – accounts you believe to be accurate -- are largely a result of your interpretation of events at the time they took place, and your memory of them long after the fact.

Your mental outlook and your maturity heavily influence your interpretation and memories of those events.

You've just got to let that sink in.

If this is true, what are the implications?

Most importantly, it means you could choose to reinterpret, and thus revise the stories you tell yourself and they might be just as valid as the ones you've repeated and believed your entire Life.

It also means you could choose to reinterpret your stories through a more mature or optimistic lens if you're willing to do the work.

What???

Yes, you heard me right. By shifting your interpretation, or your point of view, your story could appear entirely different to you than it does now *and yet not be at odds with the facts*. By way of illustration…

Allow me to share a story about a goat! It's an example of how your point of view can alter your interpretation of Life events.

The Goat and the Motorcycle

You and I have decided to meet for a dinner date in front of an elegant hotel. As we approach each other from opposite street corners, we watch the cars zip by, waiting for a moment to safely rendezvous.

Suddenly, to our great surprise, a goat jumps out into the middle of the boulevard! A motorcycle swerves. A car skids to a stop. A second car hits the first one in the backside!

What happened? You and I both witnessed the very same event, but did we see the same thing?

Perhaps from your point of view, you could see the gate open on the truck carrying the goat and so your story begins: "First a gate opened on an old truck and a goat jumped out, looking confused. The guy in the truck was too slow to catch him, so the goat ran into the street." etc.

From my location, I could see the motorcycle coming from half a block away. "The driver must have been having trouble with his brakes. I noticed he didn't fully stop at the last intersection, so when the goat came into the street, the man was distracted and didn't have time to stop." etc.

So, here's the problem with recounting this event: If you tell your story and I tell mine, they literally cannot be the same.

If a policeman asks us to describe what caused the second car to hit the first, I might say "The motorcycle was in trouble and the driver was distracted." You might say "Someone carelessly allowed a goat to exit his truck and then couldn't catch him."

Does that make one story untrue? Both stories will be right, at least from our points of view. Perhaps some combination of the two stories would come closer to the truth of the matter. Pity the poor policeman, whose job is to decide who's at fault!

What happened in this tale of the goat and the motorcycle is not so different from how we construct our beliefs and personal life stories.

We witness events. We have emotional experiences as part of those events. We have a point of view about them. We believe our own point of view and repeat it to ourselves and to others, sometimes for decades. We rarely check in with anyone else to see if his or her perception of events jives with our own.

My sister Helen can vouch for this. On many occasions, we've had conversations about our childhood. As we reminisce, inevitably she'll recall the circumstances quite differently than I do. "That's not how it happened!" is often heard emanating from our conversations! Does this happen in your family, too? Importantly, many of our beliefs originate in early family events.

REVELATIONS: The Children's Sculpture Garden

When I was a dance educator, I had the good fortune of teaching in public schools throughout Kentucky in residencies funded by the Kentucky Arts Council and the National Endowment for the Arts. My primary subject was Creative Movement. In this context, I often used a game to teach children about the topic you and I've been discussing! *The Sculpture Game* was a way to show children that our perception of everything we see is influenced by the point of view from which we observe it.

I divided the children into two groups of around 15 each. One group was called the "The Observers," and the other "The Sculpture Builders." The sculpture builders came into the center of the room, one at a time, and then froze in a shape of their choice. As each new child entered the space, she joined the others in some thoughtful, intentional way, also freezing in a shape of some kind. Options included physically attaching themselves to each other through touch, imitating each other's shapes, or doing something opposite to the others.

The entire time each child continued to hold his frozen shape! (This is not easy by the way). The 15-person sculptures that arose from this exercise were often complex and satisfying visually. Some were compact and condensed; others were sprawling and covered half the gymnasium. Many were funny!

The second part of the exercise was for the observer group to slowly walk around the periphery of the space, examining the sculpture in the center of the room made from the other team's 'frozen' bodies. As they moved around the sculpture, I would ask them to pause and look at the sculpture and to notice how it changed as they stood in different positions in the room. I'd ask them provocative questions like: "Where are the windows in the shape, the straight and curved lines? Do you see any repetition? Are some people visible now who you couldn't see before? Does the shape have a meaning from this viewpoint?" Among other things, I always hoped this exercise would plant a seed in the young minds: "Does this mean that your assessment of Life events is influenced by where you're standing? Does everyone else see things the same way you do?"

Want to experience the sculpture game effect for yourself? I posted photos of a famous Rodin sculpture from the Hirshhorn Museum and Sculpture Garden in Washington, D.C.. to simulate the game for you. ☺ Visit LifeForceMarketing.com/MORE

Practices for Changing Beliefs and Stories

The obvious questions are: "When you notice the appearance of negative beliefs and stories, how should you respond?" and "What can you do next?"

If you're so inclined, you can embark on a methodical process of revising them.

Don't go on a fool's errand.

Let's establish one thing. There's no point in getting upset with yourself when you notice undermining thoughts creeping in, lurking in the corners of your mind. Why beat yourself up? It's almost never helpful.

I also don't recommend trying to stop having your negative thoughts. Even though they can indeed undermine your ability to move forward, trying to get rid of them is a fool's errand. They are initially just a part of the way your mind is accustomed to operating. Don't take it personally! If you engage in a mind-training process such as meditation or the methods I'm suggesting here, you'll see fewer undermining thoughts eventually. It's doubtful they'll ever go away completely; however, you'll be less dominated by them.

Instead, let's take a friendlier and more realistic approach. What if you could learn to recognize your undermining, fearful thoughts for what they are? What if you understood that these thoughts are the product of an old unconscious belief system? What if you *knew* that your thoughts are a product of mind activity and not a reflection on you as a person? Would this recognition drain the undermining beliefs of their power?

Let's find out by doing some belief work.

The Rev. Michael Beckwith said in one of his sermons at Agape International Spiritual Center recently, "In order to move into new territory, you're gonna have to let something go."

It is entirely possible to let go of our interpretations of the past, loosening the stranglehold that old beliefs, self-images, and stories have been having on us. The rewards for doing so are incalculable. So, let's get started.

> "You are not responsible for the programming you picked up in childhood. However, as an adult, you are one hundred percent responsible for fixing it."
>
> Ken Keyes, Jr.

As I mentioned earlier, there are many ways of altering embodied old beliefs. The process we'll work with here is a simple and effective one influenced by the work of Mary Morrissey, Chogyam Trungpa, Moshe Feldenkrais and Werner Erhard. There are more in-depth forms of belief work that I teach my coaching clients for making lasting change. The method I'm sharing here is something you can begin using immediately.

To shift your perspective and revise your stories, you can do four things, and do them frequently, until this robust process becomes a habit. Here are your instructions for a process I call NEDS.

For Your Immediate Use...
NEDS: Notice, Experience, Detach, Shift

▪ NOTICE

Notice when an old story is popping up, demanding to be heard, compromising your actions and sucking the air out of your dreams. You may first notice it as a thought. However, it's just as likely it will show up as some kind of physical accompaniment to the thought, such as: tightening in the jaw, queasiness in the belly, an unexplained mood shift, the onset of vague boredom or depression, tightness in the neck, a furrowed brow, tension in the facial muscles, restlessness, a nagging headache, or other symptoms that seem to have appeared for no particular reason.

Although it seems like just noticing something should be easy as pie – almost a non-event -- it's a significant milestone. Once you're able to notice your reactions, *while they're happening*, you're already halfway to lowering the impact the old story has on you. As Mary Morrissey often reminds her students: "Notice what you're noticing." Let this be your mantra.

▪ EXPERIENCE

This step is also misleading in its simplicity: Take a moment and experience what you've noticed.

Experiencing something is not the same as judging or rejecting it. Now is not the time to berate yourself for the thoughts you've noticed. It's a time to BE with your experience, including the headache or tiredness, tension in your jaw or hands, unhappiness in the pit of your stomach -- the physical side of what's happening.

What does 'experiencing something' mean?

Experiencing something, without judgment or analysis, is an action in itself, but it's not an action that's highly prized or often taught in Western culture. We are a culture of doers. Experiencing something falls more into the realm of 'being' than 'doing.'

To experience something, we simply sit with it, observe it. "Oh, there's that neck tension again. Let me see what that feels like." "Hmmm... there's an interesting mood passing through me. Is this mood also appearing somewhere in my body?"

When I took the Erhard Seminar Training, repeatedly, in the 80's, one of the most wondrous things I learned was related to experiencing. Werner Erhard, founder of the training usually referred to as the est training, taught that when we notice the moments in our lives, whether those moments are pleasurable or unpleasant, just by the very process of watching them -- without resisting what we're seeing, without fighting against or arguing with them -- we naturally move on to the next moment. The accompanying flip side of that teaching is that whatever we resist, persists. This is so important that it deserves two quotes ☺

> "Whatever you are pushing against, you are stuck to."
>
> Werner Erhard

> "Whatever you fight, you strengthen, and what you resist, persists."
>
> Eckhart Tolle

So, here's the practice: Don't push against what you notice, just be with it for a moment, have the experience, even if it's unpleasant.

- DETACH

The next part of your practice is to detach. Non-judgmentally, gently, detach from what you've noticed. 'Detaching' is a term often used in Buddhist teachings, in which we let go of our emotional attachment to something. Quite naturally, when we notice something hurtful, it would be easy to become caught up in the emotional content. After all, we have embodied these stories, and they are the results of our interpretation of sometimes powerful past experiences. It's easy to start 'building a paragraph around them,' building up emotional steam – becoming attached.

I'm not suggesting here that you reject your feelings or make a judgment of your emotions. Quite the contrary. Instead, the idea is to gently separate from the emotional tumult and attempt to look at the story as if you were a witness rather than a participant, adopting a slightly more detached point of view. Doing so can prevent you from falling into a rabbit hole and getting lost in your emotions.

Consider this: Deepak Chopra teaches that you are NOT the thought but the thinker of the thought. Adopting his perspective might make it easier for you to witness yourself and detach from your old stories with less self-judgment and emotional chaos. You are not the thought, but the thinker of the thought.

Detaching takes a lot of intention and is a powerful practice in its own right. While learning, it can help to have a coach or meditation instructor working beside you.

Change your frame of mood: Imagine that your thoughts are floating on a moving stream.

Another way to play with your thoughts is to imagine they are floating on a body of water, continually moving downstream until they gradually disappear. As you know, the water in a stream or river will continue to flow unless something gets in its way. Similarly, the only way that our thoughts stick around is if we put an obstacle in the stream, damming the thoughts so they can no longer flow. What do we do that places a dam in the stream of our thoughts? We attach and resist. We get upset, over-analyze, regret, or blame someone else for the thought. As we learn to observe our thoughts and their accompanying sensations, they will pass away on their own, naturally.

Try it! Often, you'll sense your physical sensations, and your frame of mood, change right on the spot.

▪ SHIFT

Finally, shift your attention to a version of your story that you want to cultivate now and in the future. Mary Morrissey likens this to changing the channel on a TV set. Switch channels, look at something else. Do this on purpose. Over time you'll get very good at it!

Good news! Because you have developed a technicolor Vision, you'll have a new channel to switch to, which is why Envisioning and Revising go hand in hand.
Many people use affirmations in this way, replacing old words with new words. Others prefer to re-visit their Vision by calling up a vivid picture of their imagined future, or by looking at their Vision Board. Some think of someone they love or a moment of happiness they experienced in the past.

My contributing editor has assured me that, at this point, the two wolves legend could be helpful, so let's listen in:

An old Cherokee Indian chief was teaching his grandson about life. "A fight is going on inside me," he told the young boy, "a fight between two wolves. One is evil, full of anger, sorrow, regret, greed, self-pity and false pride. The other is good, full of joy, peace, love, humility, kindness, and faith."

> "This same fight is going on inside of you, grandson…and inside of every other person on the face of this Earth."
>
> The grandson pondered this for a moment and then asked, "Grandfather, which wolf will win?"
>
> The old man smiled and replied, "The one you feed."

Mary Morrissey adds this to the story (I'm paraphrasing her here): The two wolves represent the stories we tell ourselves, about ourselves. If you starve your old pessimistic stories and feed your new positive stories, then the old ideas will start withering away, allowing your Vision to take over.

> "And what is it exactly that we are we feeding them? Our attention. What we choose to give our attention to will thrive."
>
> Mary Morrissey, Life Mastery Institute

It's not necessary or possible to completely rid ourselves of negative thoughts. Instead, when they pop up, we notice their presence and refuse to feed them. We starve them of our attention. We shift our focus back to our Vision and get on with Life.

The more you work with this process, the easier it will become.

Speaking personally, when I'm able to step back with just a smidgeon of detachment, I can see the stories I've told myself about myself — some true, some patently false — and how those stories have made me who I am, ever since I was old enough to think. In questioning whether these stories are true or not, I feel more in charge of my Life almost immediately.

The more you live in the present, perched on the edge between who you are now and who you're becoming, the more Life Force you will have available for creating what you want.

Making this a Life habit is invaluable for anyone with the intention of building a more lucrative, satisfying business or making other Life-altering changes in the direction of greater prosperity.

So, that's the NEDS Process, Simple and Profound. Notice, Experience, Detach, and Shift.

The NEDS process can be likened to a meditation practice.

If you've ever studied meditation, or if you have a regular meditation practice, you'll see similarities in what we just discussed to something you've learned before.

Typically, meditation practice goes like this: You start with something to focus on: a word, image, candle flame, mandala, your breathing, or a sacred sound. You notice when you have a thought that takes you in another direction; and then, gently, you shift your attention back to the object of meditation.

You may have previously assumed, as many people do, that meditation is a lot more complicated than that. There are more complex meditations, to be sure, but in the beginning, almost everyone begins with an object of meditation and a practice of training the mind to return to the object. (I extend apologies to my long-time meditator friends who may feel I haven't done this vast subject justice.)

Although the steps in meditation, and in revising your personal stories alike, are simple – they're by no means easy! Honestly, until you have the habit in place, sometimes it feels like a great, frustrating bore to keep coming back to the object of meditation, or shifting your attention back to your Vision, again and again! It can seem like hard work at first. Rest assured, with practice you can become more adept.

In meditation, and in the 'revising' process, too, you will gradually learn that there's no point in getting frustrated just because, for the 100th time, you're thinking again about your lunch, your irritating neighbor, next year's trip to the ocean, the shortcomings of your siblings, the new jacket you saw in the store window, that time you failed algebra or got fired, or how much you want a donut right now. Instead, you recognize this for what it is – THINKING -- and then you let it go. You detach from it and its emotional content, and you shift your attention back to your object of meditation -- or to the Vision of the business you're determined to build. Change the channel, again and again.

Becoming more comfortable with the NEDS process is one of a hundred good reasons to include meditation practice in your daily regimen.

One More Practice: Cultivating a New 'Frame of Mood' by Feeling the Future

I'd like to share one more aspect of the NEDS process with you. When it's time to Shift your attention, shift it to, not only the images of your Vision, but also the feeling of them. Allow me to explain.

Contrary to popular propaganda, you have a great deal of influence over not only your frame of mind but also your frame of mood! Unless you're living in profoundly difficult circumstances (such as starvation, extreme pain or loss), you have the potential to live in the *feeling* of your Vision all day, every day.

Living in the feeling of what you desire not only changes your frame of mood, it is the secret sauce of manifesting what you want and revising the story you tell yourself about yourself.

> "Appreciation in advance brings everything you want to you."
>
> Abraham Hicks

Instructions:

In the present, conjure up the feeling you would have if your Life and your business were already just as you have envisioned.

How would you feel? Can you imagine what your mood would be like? How about bodily sensations? Would your shoulders drop or your neck relax? Would a smile appear on your face, or your eyes light up? Would you feel a surge of optimism?

Is it possible for you to put yourself in that frame of mood while you walk around in today's reality?

Perhaps this sounds like a ridiculous magic trick I'm asking you to undertake. I understand why you might see it that way. I can only ask you to try it for yourself.
Here's an example of what I'm suggesting:

> Let's imagine you're at your computer working on an e-book you're writing to promote your practice. You have a clear Vision of what you're doing and how this e-book will help you reach your prospective clients. You're focused on the Vision of all the good that can come out of this work, so your frame of mood is upbeat and optimistic. You feel happy in mind and body. Continuing your work, firmly grounded in the present, you're living in the mood of what it will feel like to achieve your goals.

Then, out of the blue, your mind skips a beat and lands on worrisome thoughts. Your thinking may say: "But what will my peers think about this? Will it be good enough? How will I know what to do next? Are you sure this is a good idea?"

These thoughts trigger a different mood! You start to fall into the rabbit hole of Self-Doubt.

VOILA! Then you Notice what's happened. You say something to yourself like, "Hey! I've slipped into a bad mood! Let's get out of here!"

Then you Shift your attention back to the *feeling* of upbeat optimism about your e-book and how others will receive it in the future. Soak it in. Remind yourself for a few seconds of your Vision. Feel it as clearly and viscerally as possible, as if this future you're imagining were already happening.

And then get back to your e-book. That's the practice!

Since I began studying with Abraham Hicks in 2013, I've been enthralled by the practice of feeling the future, appreciating in advance. I've found several reliable ways of putting myself in the feeling of my envisioned future, and the one I like best is remembering a previous experience in which I felt elated, satisfied, excited, gratified, or joyous. One of these reliable memories is of the Woodland Dance Festival.

REVELATIONS: Remembering Pride, Joy, and Victory

At the height of my dance career, I founded an annual festival called the Woodland Dance Festival. It was an idea that sprang from nothingness, sprouted into form in my imagination, and finally matured into a full-blown reality. A Day of Outdoor Dance… that was what it was meant to be and was – but that simple tagline doesn't begin to tell what occurred in Lexington's Woodland Park on the last Sundays in September from 1984 to 1989. The Festival was co-sponsored by the parks department and our dance company, Syncopated, Inc.

When I first imagined it, I began to see things that could happen in the Park, things that hadn't happened before. As a modern and experimental dancer with an interest in site-specific choreography, creating a series of events that would use the entire park was a thrilling prospect. Site-specific choreography demands taking a look at the structures and landscape, the key features and hidden treasures in a specific environment and responding to them in some way utilizing your art form.

Woodland Park, in those days, had a rich variety of spaces, including a softball field, an Olympic swimming pool, and much more. Over the six years of the Festival, we used every nook and cranny of that park, and many thousands of people attended.

> When I want to call up the feelings of victory and profound satisfaction in the work I've done, I remember riding around in my golf cart on Festival days, watching it unfold as planned. I recall the imaginative and mind-blowing things dancers and other artists were doing in the Park and the smiles on the faces of the audience as they circulated from one event to another.
>
> This memory ALWAYS makes me feel a thrill from head to toe. It fills me with an effervescent pride and gratitude that seems to seep out of my pores and light up my countenance.

Vividly recalling the Woodland Dance Festival gives me a means of imagining, viscerally, what my future accomplishments will feel like. This practice fills me with optimism, every time.

What moments in your Life could you recall that would flood you with feelings of pride and positive expectation? Seriously, stop and think about it!

Now, for a Quick Review

Notice when an old story is trying to re-assert itself. You can tell this is happening because you'll notice that you're judging yourself mercilessly, comparing yourself to others, feeling off balance emotionally, or perhaps feeling hopeless or bored about the future. As soon as you notice these clues, acknowledge what's happening, experience the moment without resistance, and shift your attention back to your Vision.

Consciously, purposely conjure up the mood of your Vision once again. Remind yourself how electrifying it will feel to have the things you've envisioned transpire.

At first, you may have some resistance to this process. You might even think it's easier to surrender to the old stories in which you feel sorry for yourself, resent others, sell yourself short, worry incessantly or ignore your desires. (I'm not trying to insult you; we're all in this together). Persistence is the essential commitment.

And in This Way, Your Stories Will Change.

Cultivate the ability to feel the future; take authority over your frame of mood and see what happens. Become adept at noticing, experiencing, detaching and shifting your attention. As you become untethered from more of the junk thinking, the stories you tell yourself about yourself will change. They will no longer carry the same emotional charge. More often than not, you'll have access to an expansive feeling of inner freedom. Your Life Force will flow more freely; you'll feel more alive.

Do you remember the personal beliefs I shared with you at the beginning of this chapter? Here's a refresher:

- Sophisticated, well-educated people don't value small town girls from Kentucky.
- I'm under-educated and inferior to those with more education or who have seen more of the world than I.
- I am lazy and don't do the work needed to excel.
- Because of the way some people treated me as a young girl, I didn't have high self-esteem as a young woman, and thus I'm not as successful as I should be.

By working with the techniques described here, and many others, I've changed most of that story so that only rarely do I see these beliefs popping up. And, when I do, I know how to turn them around. My revised story goes something like this:

- Being a small-town girl from Kentucky has given me advantages. My values are grounded in a strong relationship with community and the Earth. I was free to roam without constant supervision. I lived in an environment where no one locked their doors, and everyone knew everyone, giving me a basic feeling of safety in the world.

- Because I had less formal education than I had initially intended, I have remained open to learning and have been highly educated by Life. I have the confidence to ask good questions and learn from people who are more knowledgeable than I on specific topics. I'm confident of my intellectual abilities.

- I have proven by my actions that I'm not lazy. I've shown great initiative throughout my Life. I'm an accomplished person with an admirable work ethic.

- Although my upbringing included frightening and emotionally devastating experiences, I also grew up with positive influences that still shape the Life I'm living. The things I've overcome have made me strong, self-reliant, and empathic.

To learn more about turning your story around, visit www.LifeForceMarketing.com/MORE

How will you re-write your story as you examine your beliefs and free yourself from their undermining influences?

I'd love to hear from you.

What's next? Now you've done some envisioning and been introduced to a technology for revising mind habits that could block the door to your prosperity. Let's move on to one more aspect of the inner game of marketing: Remembering Your Resources. You're gonna love it!

Here's something you can do right now.

A simple, easy practice for shifting attention!

Recalling that Mary Morrissey likens shifting attention to changing the channels of a TV set, let's practice turning your thoughts in the direction of your choosing.

- Think about Someone you love. Visualize the face, the voice, the laughter, the personality and the body of this person.
- Think about the last time you interacted with him or her.
- Notice that, even though it's fun to think about this person, your mind also wants to think about other stuff.
- Take a moment and instead of fighting the mind about this habit of leaping about, notice the thoughts your mind is producing.
- To do this, you'll shift even more into the present moment.
- Go back to thinking about Someone you love once again.
- Now, think about another person in your Life, someone you find irritating.
- Recall the last time they irritated you.
- Notice the emotions and bodily sensations that arise.
- Stay with this for a minute longer, simply experiencing it all.
- Now go back to thinking about Someone you love again.
- Feel the love you have for her or him.
- See where you feel this love in your body.
- Now notice the feeling of exactly where you are at this precise moment.
- Which parts of your body are touching the ground, or a chair or bed.
- How heavy or light do you feel? How upright or slumped?
- Tune in with all of your available attention to this felt sense of yourself.

This activity is an example of a method for developing mental flexibility. Discover that you are not the thought but the thinker of the thought and that you have the power to change the channel any time you want.

Celebrate every victory! Celebrate taking the time to notice how you feel. Celebrate looking anew at the stories you tell yourself. Celebrate having made it through what may have been a challenging chapter!

Find excellent examples of belief work done by my coaching clients on our site, used with permission, anonymously. LifeForceMarketing.com/MORE

Remember

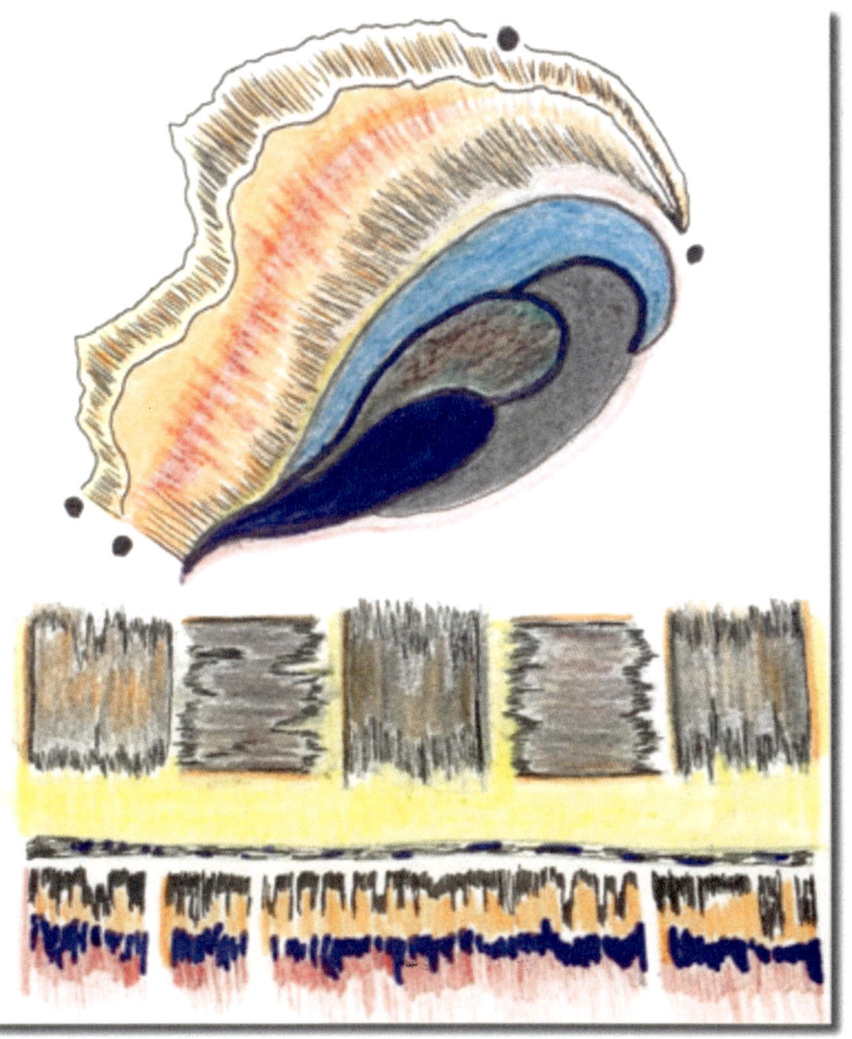

Start with where you are, with what you have;
you always have way more
than you recognize.

Mary Morrissey

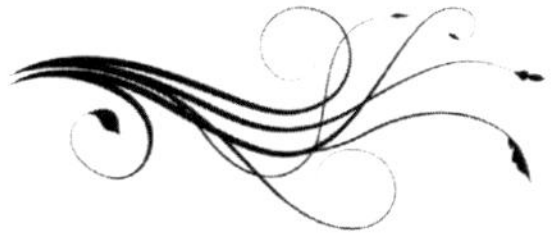

Step 3
Remember Your Resources: a Fresh Way of Looking at Assets

When we think about 'assets,' we usually think about money, investments, and property. Those are certainly assets, important ones that can help us get where we're going if we know how to use them well. However, there are many other kinds of assets, which we'll call 'resources' for purposes of this discussion. Some of these resources are tangible, and many are intangible.

In this chapter, you'll have the chance to recognize and remember resources you've been gathering throughout your Lifetime. We'll focus primarily on your intangible assets. Identifying them now will come in handy as you move through later chapters.

Good Will is a familiar intangible asset.

Many businesses have succeeded or failed on the basis of something intangible known as Good Will. Good Will is essentially the value of a company's reputation, including its relationship with its customers. Good Will is something that a business can take a long time to build up but can lose in a heartbeat by doing something dishonest or unethical or failing to meet the quality standards that its customers have come to expect. It's difficult to assign monetary worth to this type of resource, but that doesn't make it any less important. You also have other intangible resources that are difficult to put a price tag on but are nonetheless valuable. It's easy to overlook their importance. I'd be willing to bet you have many intangible resources that you haven't identified as business assets!

Identifying the resources you bring to the table for building a more successful business can open your eyes to options you may have missed otherwise.

Here are a few examples of resources/assets that could have a positive impact on your business in one way or another:

- Friends or peers who can refer new clients to you
- A good track record with your former clients and peers
- Training and credentials or specialized areas of expertise
- Thank you notes or testimonials
- Exceptional interviewing or listening skills
- A knack for putting others at ease
- A list of previous clients, a mailing list or social media following
- Groups you belong to, either in person or online
- High quality photographs representing your work
- A talent for being on camera or expressing yourself well in a public setting
- The ability to talk about your work to one person at a time
- A good credit rating, savings account or line of credit
- Good intuition; a strong connection to spirit
- A good sense of humor
- The support of your family
- Professional friends who will give you honest feedback
- A business license, well-chosen business name or logo
- A business checking account or telephone line
- A friend or acquaintance who serves the same sort of clients you do but provides a non-competing service
- Equipment and supplies, including your computer, printer and smart phone
- Previous experience in another business that may be relevant
- Personal qualities such as resiliency, innovativeness and persistence
- Relationships with people of influence in your community
- The patience and other qualities and skills earned from being a parent
- Personal traits such as generosity, empathy, or clear-headedness, optimism
- An active imagination
- A history of successes
- Writing skills or a strong sense of design
- Organizational skills
- An engaging personality or demeanor that generates trust in others
- A family member's income supporting you while you build your business
- The goodwill of your current and past clients
- Courage and self-confidence!
- Experience with persevering when difficulties and obstacles arise
- A clear understanding of the problems your potential clients are experiencing
- Traits and skills you acquired through your various roles in life

You may be wondering: Why should I take the time to think about my Resources when we're supposed to be learning about holistic marketing and building a prosperous business? A few reasons...

1. There is a surprising intersection of your resources and your Vision. As you realize how resourced you already are, your Vision will become more vivid, possibly more detailed, and may seem increasingly plausible.

2. Reviewing and deep-mining your resources will subtly shift your impression of yourself, even increasing your self-confidence for new projects.

3. Having a clear understanding of your resources will help you compose your marketing language (as you'll see in Step 5: COMPOSE).

4. Knowing more about your resources can influence your strategy for an overall promotion plan (as you'll see in Step 7: SELECT).

Sometimes the simplest thing can make a significant difference.

REVELATIONS: 52 Posts on Facebook, a remembering exercise

I wouldn't have had the courage to write the book in your hands if I hadn't first delved into my resources comprehensively.

The exercise began as an idea to write 52 Facebook posts before Labor Day in 2015, each on the subject of WORK. I made this decision on a whim after a friend made 60 consecutive posts on Facebook honoring her upcoming 60th birthday. (*Thank you, Karen Rose.*) Something about this idea -- a series of posts on a single subject -- interested me. Labor Day was 52 days away, so...

I began by writing about my first job, babysitting, and discovered an important lesson that's served me ever since – how to ask for money. As I continued to move through the chronology of a road-less-traveled work life, I realized repeatedly there were lessons being learned, challenges being faced, wins and losses with each new experience. With the encouragement of Facebook friends, I continued to write. This 52-day project took me back into memories of my past, invited me to recall people, places, and events.

I realized that I had collected a plethora of resources through my long and varied work Life. I wrote about working in thoroughbred racing, adventure retreat production, choreography and dance education, school bus driving, magazine editing, therapeutic bodywork, waiting tables, and network marketing. In revisiting my past, I felt a growing appreciation for myself! Many regrets I had previously held faded away as I looked at them through the less judgmental, more generous point of view of an experienced adult. By the time I got to Labor Day, I had changed the story I tell myself, about myself, forever.

Conducting this exhaustive look at my work life caused a new self-image to emerge, partly because I saw for the first time the many and varied resources I had developed along the way; how capable I had become.

Just a few of the resources I discovered through this writing project are:

- Because I have been asked many times to take on tasks and duties for which I received no training, I am good at figuring things out on my own. These do-it-yourself lessons have given me a strong feeling of self-reliance.
- I have a lot of experience with changing careers. I began to wonder, "Maybe that's something I can help others with."
- Not only did I enjoy writing about my professional life, but many people enjoyed reading about it too. An idea emerged: "Perhaps I have what it takes to write a book…"
- I've had a wealth of on-the-job training in adapting to different kinds of people, which made me suitable for later jobs in multi-cultural environments.

To tell you everything I received from this project would entail writing another book altogether, and I plan to do that one day, but I hope you get the idea!

I have never returned to a lesser view of myself since.

More importantly, a much simpler form of this exercise, making a list of your resources, can make a big difference for you, too. For instance, let me tell you about Willow.

Willow, who is someone I work with as a prosperity and marketing coach, had an eye-opening and joyful experience while making a list of her resources. She writes books and teaches classes in shamanism and breath work. Some examples of what she discovered:

- She remembered she had been collecting stories, interviews, and recordings about Shamanistic practices since she was a teenager. She's now beginning to incorporate these materials into her present work.
- She remembered a box of positive thank you letters she had received from group classes conducted several years ago, letters she is now using as a source of testimonials for her brochure and website.
- She re-discovered her love for interviewing people, experienced in a sociology class she had taken in college, and realized she could use those skills to be more effective in her intake process with new clients. Using those interviewing skills more intentionally could increase her client retention rates.

That's why, in the *Here's Something You Can Do Right Now* exercise at the end of this chapter, I'm asking you to write a list of YOUR resources.

I know from working with clients who have gone through a similar process how very transformative this exercise can be.

Here's something you can do right now.

Make your Resource List. Here are a few specific prompts to get you going. Don't be shy about going deep! This list is just for you.

- List training and education you've completed or begun, including that which doesn't pertain to your current field.
- List organizations, offline and online, with which you're affiliated.
- List the people in your sphere right now who could become your clients.
- "You're good at that!" Is there something your friends mention repeatedly?
- List the roles you have played and the traits and skills you've acquired. For example, by being a parent, you may have acquired characteristics such as patience, kindness, persistence, tolerance for the errors of others, plus abilities to multi-task, engage in imaginative play, stay on schedule, and plan ahead.
- What are the traits and skills you have acquired as a result of being an:
  - elementary, high school or college student, neighbor, sibling
  - athlete, dancer, Feldenkrais student or yoga practitioner
  - activist, caretaker, church-goer, or community leader
  - gardener, cook, nurse, household budget manager, or reunion organizer
  - Girl Scout leader, meditation instructor, or Sunday School teacher
  - deep sea diver, equestrian, world traveler, kickboxer, singer, musician
  - high school yearbook editor or human resources manager

- Applaud yourself for all that you've become. Count each area of growth as an individual resource and write them all down.

- After you've made a list, pause. Take a few minutes to feel gratitude for everything you have on your list. Notice your frame of mood.

- Celebrate every victory! Celebrate remembering something about yourself that you respect. Celebrate being more resourced than you may have realized.

part two

Initiating Vital Actions

Choose the people you want as your clients. Compose compelling stories that will resonate with them and genuinely represent who you are. Select strategies to spread your stories so the people who are looking for you can find you. Then you'll be ready to Build your marketing infrastructure.

When you make a choice,
you change the future.

Deepak Chopra

Step 4
Choose the People You Want to Serve and the Problems You Can Help Them Solve

The best marketing begins with soul-searching. I love that sentence. It appeals to me because it describes in very few words one of the basic premises of holistic marketing.

It provides a reminder that it makes no sense to go bounding into the world with a new website, setting up interviews and attending networking events UNTIL you know what you're trying to accomplish and how to tell a story about yourself that's based on a current sense of reality rather than a belief system leftover from your childhood.

Because you've probably had some interest in doing inner work long before you encountered our book, everything you've learned thus far may have had a familiar ring to it. At the very least, since you're in a business that, in one way or another, transforms people's lives, you already know something about the inner game.

Still, you may be wondering what all this soul-searching has to do with building your prosperous practice. I think it will become clear over time as we journey together through the OUTER elements of marketing. Let's get started!

In this chapter you can expect to learn about:

- Why you should choose a target audience

- Choosing a niche market you want to serve and understand the problems they have that you can solve
- Identifying and getting to know your Ideal Client
- Figuring out where to find your Ideal Clients

A clarifying note on language:
To a certain extent, the terms 'target audience,' 'niche,' 'tribe' and 'Ideal Client' all refer to the same person or group of persons – the people you will direct your marketing efforts toward, the people you want to work with and become an expert at serving. I've used all four terms interchangeably. I suggest you think of these terms as all referring to the same thing. In a very practical sense, they are.

Why You Should Choose a Target Audience

Let's begin by talking about target audiences and why choosing one is something that will benefit you.

You've probably heard this term 'target audience' before. This may be one of the marketing terms that you don't relate to, either because you have no earthly idea who your target audience is or because the idea of 'targeting' someone reinforces everything you don't like about the whole business of marketing.

It's also possible that you're a card-carrying member of the "My Work is Good for Everyone Club."

In other words, you may find it difficult to think about a specific kind of person you'd like to serve because you know in your heart of hearts that just about anyone who experiences your work will benefit.

I understand, I really do. Having spent decades as a dance educator, massage therapist, and later as a Feldenkrais Practitioner and Bones for Life teacher, I know from experience I can help many different sorts of people with a wide range of problems. For that reason (and because I didn't know better!), for a long time, I found it almost impossible to choose a target audience. My attitude was: I'm open to everyone.

And here's what I want you to know: Being open to everyone isn't the same thing as marketing to everyone.

I'll use my own previous career as an example. In the beginning, I was open to sharing my skills with everyone and made no attempt to choose a target audience. I wasn't as busy as I wanted to be. Some years ago, this changed for the better when I began targeting a particular Ideal Client. As a result, I got the practice I wanted. Working with this target audience brought me a lot of satisfaction.

My target audience was senior women 60 and over who have worked hard to stay active and healthy but are struggling with the impacts of gravity and aging.

It's important to them to keep moving, move well and easily, and to become more self-aware. They want to feel as young as possible for as long as possible. They want to reduce their aches and pains, feel optimistic about aging. Many of our lessons focused on how to sit, stand and walk, reach for the high shelf, roll over in bed, walk the dog without injury, pull weeds, lift grandchildren, get down on the floor and back up again – practical matters of concern to aging adults.

Choosing this Ideal Client allowed me to narrow and refine my message. Because I began specializing in one type of client, I was better able to understand their problems and was nearly always able to offer them helpful solutions. That's what happens when you have a target audience. That's what I want to show you how to do in this chapter.

Now that I'm working as a holistic marketing coach, my focus is on writing books and building a coaching practice -- so now I have a completely different target audience!

REVELATIONS: *Being Open* to Everyone is Not the Same as *Marketing* to Everyone

The first time I heard the term 'target audience' was while recruiting a new board member for a dance organization I was working with: Syncopated, Inc.

We were an ambitious and highly creative organization with big ideas but limited human and financial resources. We were trying to expand our board of directors to include more 'business-minded' people, and I was trying to recruit a stockbroker named Lawrence. When I met him at his office, the first words out of his mouth were, "Who is your target audience?"

I was fully unprepared to answer Lawrence coherently, and I felt embarrassed. I recall telling this savvy prospective new supporter that we didn't have a target audience, that we were "open to everyone." Being open to everyone was a point of pride for us since part of Syncopated, Inc.'s mission was to bridge the gaps between different kinds of people through dance and music.

I didn't know at the time that *being open* to everyone is not the same as *marketing* to everyone.

It was many years later before I understood the significance of the fact that I, and my partners, hadn't given any serious thought to who we were trying to reach and attract. We were so naïve; we believed that everyone was interested in dance! I laugh about it now, but at the time it was serious.

Because I loved that organization, the people in it, the breathtaking work we did, and everything it stood for, I wish I'd known then what I know now! If we could have answered Lawrence's question about our target audience more thoughtfully, we might have been savvier in our recruitment of board members, contributors, volunteers, performers, and students. Because we targeted everyone and didn't know how to tailor our message to the specific kinds of people who would be drawn to our work and esthetic, we undoubtedly missed out on valuable opportunities.

I now understand the difference between being open to everyone and marketing to everyone -- and I know that choosing a niche almost always brings new opportunity.

One of my mentors, Bill Baren, talks about choosing a target audience – your niche or tribe – and how it opens you up to new levels of success in your business:

"When you focus your business on the right (profitable) niche,
- Ideal clients seek you out, eager to work with you;
- Your niche is something (for which) you become known as an expert;
- Your income increases because it's easier to attract the right clients;
- You get invited to speak for awesome audiences...;
- Marketing and growing your business becomes easy;
- You get a lot more word-of-mouth (clients) and referrals."

Bill Baren Coaching

Please believe me. You. Must. Choose.

Essentially, the primary reason for choosing an Ideal Client is that it's much easier marketing to one kind of person than to every kind of person.

Put another way, it's an adage in marketing circles that if you're marketing to everyone, you're probably reaching no one.

Just between you and me, aren't there some kinds of clients who, although you could probably help them, you don't really want to? Aren't there clients that you *love love love* working with and wish would come in greater numbers? Being honest with yourself about who you enjoy working with and who you don't will help with your decision-making.

Choosing a target audience will increase your sense of inner authority because you'll literally be creating your own business. That's why you're in business for yourself, isn't it?

The feeling of "being at cause in the matter" – making the relevant decisions to create the business you want rather than merely accepting what comes your way -- will also grow your self-confidence. Being at cause in the matter will put you more closely in touch with your Life Force.

p.s. "Being at cause in the matter" is a term coined by Werner Erhard in the 1980's. He was the founder of Erhard Seminar Trainings, also known as **est.**

Sometimes, after you've already been in business for awhile, you might begin to narrow the scope of your clientele – even if you haven't formally chosen a target audience yet. That's what happened to me.

REVELATIONS: A problem that is not mine to solve

The first time I narrowed my focus as a holistic practitioner was when, as a massage therapist, I realized I wasn't very affective at working with the problem of Sciatica. Although I knew the protocols and was a highly skillful therapist for many other conditions, I finally admitted to myself that I didn't feel confident working with Sciatica. I made a decision: "I don't want to accept these clients anymore. I'll refer them to someone I know who is brilliant in this area." This was a big turning point for me.

I had been reluctant to make this change because I kept thinking my results would improve. I thought admitting my deficiency would mean I had failed. My modus operandi was to accept almost every kind of client who came my way, so 'giving up' a whole group of people wasn't natural for me. However, once I made the decision, I immediately felt a sense of relief and pride. I was being honest with myself about my strengths and weaknesses. I was acting professionally by referring these clients to other practitioners. Because I did so, other bodyworkers occasionally reciprocated and referred clients to me. Most importantly, I was freeing myself from the necessity of trying to work on a problem that wasn't mine to solve. It was liberating.

From then on, I was more selective about the clients I accepted.

By that point in my career, I knew which problems I was particularly adept at solving. I understood the people who were experiencing those challenges. I knew the likely progression of their conditions – how quickly their situation would improve, what other support they would need, the activities they should avoid, etc. I began to relax into working more often with people whose problems I deeply understood, and realized I was happier when doing so.

Reaching this professional decision wasn't an overnight occurrence. It took a while. I understand, wholeheartedly, that you may not be ready to choose one kind of client today, but I ask you to consider it for yourself and for your marketing efforts.

There is one caveat.

If you're starting a brand new practice and have never done the same kind of work before, you can choose up to three rather than only one Ideal Client. It will make more work for you, but it's often not practical to pick one Ideal Client when you have minimal experience in the field.

I recently worked with several newly graduated students of health coaching programs, and in each case, it was difficult to settle on just one problem to solve because the new health coaches had simply never practiced their work before. They had no idea yet what their emphases might be in the future, but they were certain about several of their primary interests in the present. We created an umbrella marketing approach for them, allowing them to attract two or three different types of clients. This way is more difficult and time-consuming, and not something I recommend except in this type of situation.

Choosing Your Tribe

I want you to know, so you don't beat yourself up about it if you find this part of your marketing process difficult, that the majority of people DO find it challenging to choose their tribe. It's a decision that will affect everything else you do in your marketing and, obviously, in delivering your services, for years to come. No wonder it can take some time! Don't rush it.

It's often easier to do this work with someone who's experienced in choosing a niche, rather than do it all by yourself. Feedback and brainstorming with someone else can be constructive. Don't be too hard on yourself! Just keep learning and working on it.

Let's clarify: Exactly what do we mean by 'niche' or 'tribe'?

Simply put, your niche is a specific target audience or tribe of people who share common traits and also one or more painful problems – problems pressing enough to them that they'll pay someone to find solutions.

What do we mean by common traits and problems? Here's a game: I'll share a few examples of tribes and you imagine what services or products might help them! Do you think these problems are severe enough that someone would pay for a solution?

- **Young fathers** who don't know much about parenting, want to be better fathers and don't want to sit in parenting classes filled with only women.
- **Bookkeepers** who spend 8-10 hours a day in front of their computers and have developed neck and shoulder pain
- **International students** who don't have the funds to buy a car nor the time to apply for a U.S. driver's license. (Uber filled this niche and several others)
- **Mothers of disabled children** who are seriously stressed out, unable to sleep well, under-resourced, and suffering from constant worry
- **Nurses or social workers** who are burned out from the constant stress of caring for others and need an affordable way to pamper themselves.
- **Professional violin, guitar, and other string players** who suffer from shoulder and arm pain and are frustrated by how this pain is affecting the amount of time they can practice their music.

Got the idea? Common traits and problems.

Dominic Canterbury, the author of "Three Critical Elements of a Great Target," also offers a helpful way to wrap your mind around this:

> "Another way of saying this is that people in your niche are all experiencing a common situation. They're all the same kind of character in the same kind of story. If they were to sit down and talk with each other, they would be able to relate to each other's experience, finish each other's sentences... You'd hear a lot of things like, 'Oh wow! Me too! No kidding. I deal with the same thing. I know exactly what you mean!'"

Another expert point of view about niche:

To paraphrase another one of my mentors, Eben Pagan, when you're trying to clarify your niche, you want to find an unmet need, inside a group of people – a need that you can meet by creating products and services that deliver the desired results.

1. an unmet need
2. inside a group of people
3. a need that you can meet
4. by creating products and services
5. that deliver the desired results.

Eben has a multi-million-dollar enterprise teaching others to build online businesses that sell information products. But, in his earlier business life, he was doing something very different, and he often shares this story with his students.

When he first got into business, he decided to try providing dating advice. He quickly realized that most online dating advice was being written for women; there was a shortage of places men could go for advice appropriate to their needs. (1 and 2. unmet need, inside a group of people)

He decided to specialize in men. Over time, by listening to many men who had bought his products, he found out what they needed specifically in their dating lives. (3. identifying a need that he could meet)

What do you suppose was their biggest wish? Men want to be good at approaching women (or men) -- someone they're interested in dating for the first time. Over time, Eben became known as an expert in the field; he became The Go-To Person for men who want to be confident and successful in approaching potential new dating partners for the first time. (4 and 5. He created products and services that delivered the desired results)

Getting started: Ask yourself provocative questions to help you choose

- What are some of the problems people have which fall within the purview of your training, expertise, and talents?
- What kind of people do you, or would you, especially enjoy working with?
- Is there a problem out there that you could solve for which there are currently very few people providing solutions?
- Do you have an affinity for, or inside knowledge of, a particular group of people?
- Is there a group of people with whom you have a high degree of credibility?

Additional approaches to choosing your niche

A second way to get good ideas for your niche is to research the specialties of others in your field. The research process itself can stimulate ideas.

A third way, one that is especially useful for those who have existing long-time practices but have never chosen a specific tribe to work with... Ask another question: If you could be The Go-To Person in some area, the expert in a particular field, what would it be?

> "Selecting a niche can be a challenging aspect of starting and marketing a practice because you have to overcome your fears about focusing on a particular market and then make a commitment to serve that particular population. You have to be willing to let some areas go and realize that you can't serve everyone as well as you can serve a specific population."
>
> Tad Hargrave, Marketing for Hippies

Are you a visual learner? I recommend watching a few videos on the subject of 'niche' with experts such as Tad Hargrave. You'll find links to his videos on our website: LifeForceMarketing.com/MORE

Identifying and Getting to Know Your Ideal Clients

At some point, you'll want to start thinking of your tribe in more individualized and personal terms. Begin to discover your Ideal Client. As you personalize your tribe, in intimate detail, you prepare yourself to speak to prospective clients in words that will make sense to them. Once you've defined your Ideal Client, you'll be much more prepared to talk to real live people with authority about what you have to offer.

Your Ideal Client is ideal from two different perspectives:

- She or he is the kind of person you love to work with.
- She has the kinds of problems you are prepared to address.

From the first perspective, you might ask "When this person walks through my door, am I happy to see her?"

Your Ideal Client is the person who, when she walks in the door for her massage or acupuncture session, for her exercise or coaching session, his Bones for Life or voice lesson — you're glad to see him or her. When you look at your calendar, and you see this person's name, you feel happy. When you're working with them, you understand correctly what their needs are, and you know how to help them with the problems they're presenting. There's a feeling of compatibility there. Everything about working with your Ideal Client feels like a win-win situation.

That was pretty easy! Now for the second perspective.

At this time, I suggest you try to open yourself to a compassionate and in-depth understanding of how your Ideal Client is feeling and living, what they're longing for, what they're dreading, what they're aspiring to and desperately trying to leave behind, what makes them happy and what terrifies them. How are their problems impacting their Life choices? How does this get in their way? What do they long for?

Getting to know your Ideal Client isn't an intellectual exercise; it's an exercise of the heart.

When I said in the introduction to our book that holistic practitioners are engaging in a "livelihood of the heart," I was referring to this exercise. It's no small thing to understand the problems, pain, and lived experience of another person.

From a marketing perspective, discovering what moves and motivates your Ideal Client provides you with the keys to the kingdom. Knowing what he cares about, and needs will enable you to speak in a way that's meaningful to him.

We Can Apply a Simple Formula for
Learning about Your Ideal Client:

1. Learn about the challenges he's facing, that concern him.
2. Try to understand how those challenges are affecting him.
3. Think further and ask: What are the results of these challenges in his Life?

Let's practice this with a hypothetical man named Alvin.

First step: What is Alvin's challenge for which he is seeking help?

Alvin hurt himself ten years ago in a bicycle accident.
Now he has persistent back pain.

Second step: How is this challenge affecting Alvin?

He can't ride his bike anymore.
He can't sit, stand or walk for long periods of time without hurting.

Third step: What are the results of this challenge in Alvin's Life?

He has withdrawn from the cycling club and other activities he loves.
Because of this, he's lost track of several vital friendships.
He no longer thinks it's possible to travel in Italy as he had planned.
He often feels lonely, hemmed in and limited.
He's afraid his dreams for the future are going down the tubes.

A practitioner who wants to work with people like Alvin might say:

"My Ideal Clients are people who have had active lifestyles and are athletically inclined. Their activity has been cut short by accidents, surgeries or other circumstances. The threat of pain is always there, compromising their dreams of living active lives again and isolating them from their friends. Their pain has led to feelings of loneliness, limitation, and disappointment."

This Is What We Mean by a Target Audience.

Knowing your target audience will guide you in understanding what to say to attract them to your practice.

Because you understand what's going on with them, you can write Facebook posts, web pages and brochures designed to speak their language. They will recognize you as the person they've been trying to find.

As you'll see in Step 5: Composing Your Compelling Stories, it's this knowledge about Alvin's circumstances that will show you exactly how to talk to him, and others like him, about your massage, Feldenkrais, acupuncture, energy healing, occupational therapy, herbal medicine, or other means of addressing his back pain.

Eventually, the stories you tell about your work won't be full of references to 'alleviating back pain.' They won't be all about your modalities or your training. Your stories will speak about helping formerly active people who feel hemmed in and limited, about being unable to fulfill one's dreams, being cut off from activities with friends, being plagued by loneliness and disappointment.

Your stories will be about THEM, not about YOU.

Another way to say it is...

You're not only offering people massages or Bones for Life lessons, chiropractic adjustments or acupuncture treatments. What you're offering them is more freedom from pain and limitation, a renewal of their Visions, the ability to get on with the lives they want to live.

This old marketing adage says it still another way:

People have little interest in purchasing a bed.
What they want is a good night's sleep.

Where Can You Find Your Ideal Clients?

Now it's time to consider where your Ideal Clients are hanging out. As a niche, they will not only have specific traits and problems in common, but they'll probably also have common 'watering holes,' both online and offline. It's important in choosing a tribe for it to be a group of people who you can find.

That sounds overly simple, but a surprising number of people develop an idea of a tribe they'd like to work with, only to find later that there isn't a good way to locate them and share their stories. I don't want that to happen to you.

The fastest way to obtain this information may be to interview your Ideal Clients. If you already have a handful of clients who meet your newly defined criteria, ask them if they'll give you 20 minutes of their time to help you with a research project. If not, review your sphere of influence and see if you can find a few people to interview. If that fails, you can visit Facebook or Linked In, go to a group of some kind on those platforms that would likely have members of your tribe, and submit a poll or survey.

You can ask questions such as:

- What groups do you belong to offline and online?
- What kinds of social events do you attend regularly?
- Do you have favorite blogs, magazines, websites?
- Are you a member of a trade association?
- What other kinds of clubs, groups or organizations do you belong to?
- Do you attend church or some other kind of spiritual gathering?
- Where do you like to buy your groceries, clothes and self-care products?
- What do you do for fun? Are you a volunteer for any causes?
- Do you attend dance, yoga, Bones for Life, martial arts, or Pilates classes?
- Are you a member of a support group of some kind?
- Do you belong to the Y, a fitness center, sports club or gym?
- What are the stories you tell yourself about yourself when you think of the next chapter of your Life?

Once you know something about where your Ideal Clients congregate, you'll have clues about how you can reach out to them.

Here's a little challenge for you. Where might you look to find more clients like Alvin? Perhaps you would contact cycling, skiing or climbing clubs and find out who's suffered serious injuries in the past few years. You might talk to physical therapists or dance centers and, as before, ask about people whose participation is limited due to recent or chronic injuries. Where else? Rehab centers?

To see examples of target audiences and where you might expect to find them, visit LifeForceMarketing.com/MORE

You've Reached a Turning Point, Sophia.

Most likely you don't fully grasp yet how much easier your Life is going to be when you have chosen your target audience! Once you've defined your Ideal Clients, you'll be able to orient your practice around them. Once you have some ideas about where to find your Ideal Clients, you can select ways of marketing that will reach them. You'll be able to understand and become an expert at serving them. Because you've done this work, everything's about to change for the better! Celebrate!

Let's explore an example of how Sophia,
a (hypothetical) new holistic practitioner,
worked through the layers of defining her tribe.

Sophia is a former nurse who worked in hospitals for 15 years as a surgical nurse.
Two years ago, she decided it was time for a change in direction. She was nearing retirement age and wanted to do something professionally where she could focus more on helping people become healthier, rather than always working with the results of illness. Although her work had benefitted thousands of people, she had burned out in her role in traditional Western medicine. After a lot of thought, she enrolled in a world-class professional education program devoted to developing a new kind of expert: the Health Coach.

Now she's certified as a Nurse Health Coach and ready to launch a new private practice.

Sophia is highly skilled, but all of her previous work experience was as an employee. She has no experience with self-employment and doesn't know where to begin. She's an introvert and reluctant to do anything that resembles 'selling.' She has a broad range of services to offer and problems she can solve. Under the guidance of her marketing coach, she begins to think about a potential tribe.

Although there are many different kinds of clients she could help, Sophia has a particular affinity for older women, like herself, who are in the process of reinventing themselves. There's something about being with people who are starting afresh, creating meaningful next chapters later in lives that appeals to her. She knows she has a lot to offer them. A tribe begins to emerge in her thinking.

What else does she know about her potential tribe?

Sophia decides to make a list of some of the characteristics, needs, and habits of this potential tribe. Here's what she initially came up with:

- They've had substantial careers and later decided to either retire or move on to new adventures
- They're college-educated
- They're old enough that their children are no longer living with them or financially dependent on them
- After a lifetime of cooking for a family, they're sick of cooking
- Because they don't like to spend much time in the kitchen anymore, they have trouble finding delicious, healthy food to eat
- They may not have a background in natural approaches to food and eating
- They're at least mildly adventurous; otherwise, they wouldn't have the courage to start out on a whole new path
- They want to get to some of the items on their bucket list
- Many of them have a movement background in dance, sports, yoga, cycling or gymnastics from their youth that they left behind while raising their children
- Because of this they may crave getting back into a movement regimen again.

Sophia decides she wants to interview a few of her friends who happen to fit within her tribe to find out more about their problems, the effects of those problems on their lives, and also to learn more about where they hang out. She puts her list of questions together and sets up a few interviews.

She finds doing interviews is fun, and she's good at it! She learns way more than she expected.

After reviewing all this information and letting it sink in, Sophia realizes that a common problem her tribe faces is confusion around food, exercise, and weight.

While Sophia's not interested in being a weight loss consultant in the traditional sense, she knows how much she could assist her tribe by helping them look squarely at personal habits that aren't working for them. She knows she could offer them personalized guidance and encouragement and help them make a plan that works for them -- something far more effective than most of the advice they're currently receiving. She knows that at their age they may be loath to walk into a gym to talk about an eating problem with someone wearing size 4 yoga pants and 25 years their junior.

She understands that 'getting right' with food and exercise can be an empowering experience for them, and that with some success in that area they would be more confident in pursuing the items on their bucket lists.

She feels confident that, with her nursing background, she's in a position to advise them on a course of action with plenty of technical information to back her up. She thinks they would tend to trust her nursing background and assign her credibility because of it.

Sophia gets clearer about a potential tribe she would enjoy serving and problems she could address and help solve. A picture continues forming in her mind.

Here's a tip. The more your niche is like yourself, the easier it'll be for you to understand it. Don't be shy about choosing a niche of which you are a member!

Where can Sophia find her tribe?

She found from her interviews and other research that a good number of Sophia's prospective clients are hanging out in beginning exercise or yoga classes. Some are attending other courses offered in her community or reading books related to food choices, nutrition, cooking, changing personal habits, growing your food, herbal remedies, creating the body you want, fitting into the clothes you love, and more.

Many have recently visited career counselors and alumni organization advisers. Some belong to women's travel groups or church groups. She was surprised to learn that several of her interviewees shop at a particular clothing store specializing in adventure clothing for mature women. She learned about the magazines they read and the Linked In and Facebook groups they've joined. She even learned about the radio programs and a few podcasts they tune into regularly.

She realizes that many of these are examples of places where she might be able to find her tribe members and create a way to get her message across.

Sophia Combs knows quite a bit about the challenges facing her Ideal Clients. How about going a little deeper? What are the effects of these challenges, and the results in their Lives?

One of the questions Sophia asked in her interviews was "What are the stories you tell yourself about yourself when you think of the next chapter of your Life?"

She heard many answers to this provocative question, such as:

- "I'm not sure I'm capable of righting my relationship with food."
- "It's been so long since I exercised regularly, I'm afraid I'll hurt myself."
- "Why didn't I take care of this years ago? It's harder to lose weight now."
- "If I don't do something about my weight, I won't be able to travel."
- "How can I find the strength inside to get back on track?"

- "I'm afraid of what I'm doing to myself." "
- If I can't change these habits, I'll never be able to create my new Life."

Sophia learned that her prospective clients' challenges are:

They are embarking on a new lifestyle and don't know what to do next;

They are in transition and feel off-balance, outside of their comfort zones;

They don't feel confident they can change old habits about food and exercise, but yet it's a priority for them to do so.

The effects of these challenges are:

They don't feel confident that they can create the Life they're hoping for;

They're afraid of making mistakes;

They're frustrated with themselves for not solving their food and exercise problems earlier in Life; and

They think they may be too old to make the changes they want.

The results in their Lives are:

They might give up before they try;

They avoid signing up for the Zumba or modern dance class they'd like to take;

Their weight remains the same, or they gain additional weight; and

They fear chronic health problems may become a serious issue.

Sophia Combs now has enough information to begin actively marketing to the tribe she's chosen. In no time she'll start reaping the benefits and so will her clients.

But what if she had decided NOT to choose a tribe?

- She wouldn't know whom she's looking for, so how could she find them?
- If she happened to find someone who seemed like a person she'd enjoy working with, she wouldn't have the first idea what to say because she wouldn't have understood the problem, pain, and desire on an intimate enough level.

Congratulations Sophia! You've come a long way!

To Conclude: A Bit of Insider Information

I have good news. After going through the process of choosing an Ideal client/niche/tribe -- and continuing with it until you feel satisfied you've found your target audience, some very good things will begin happening to you, almost immediately.

You'll recognize the people you want to work with when you meet them.

You'll get better at answering the question, "Who are you and what do you do?"

You'll feel your optimism and sense of ownership rising.

You'll also stop trying to reach out to every tom, dick and harry — understanding that you're on a mission to work with a specific kind of person and that you don't have to be all things to all people. You'll understand the difference between being open to everyone and marketing to everyone. There's so much freedom in that!

You'll have sown seeds of new self-confidence and begin to believe you can use holistic marketing to your advantage. You'll see that you can educate the public in a targeted way that doesn't compromise your values or make you feel ickey inside.

I hope you begin today imagining all the wonderful people you'll be working with. It will bring you much closer to living the Life you would love to live, serving the people you want to, and having the prosperous practice of your dreams.

Working with your Ideal Clients will make you thankful that you do what you do and confirm on a daily basis that you're in the right occupation.

> "A niche is not defined by what you have to offer them,
> but by what they are needing;
> not by your solution, but by their problem;
> not by the relief you have to offer, but by their pain."
>
> Tad Hargrave

Now you've learned a lot about your tribe and your Ideal Client. In the next chapter, we'll look into how you can compose messages that speak persuasively to them. You'll see how -- because it will be evident that you understand their needs -- your prospective clients will recognize you as the professional they've been hoping to find. Let's move forward to: Step 5: Composing Your Compelling Stories.

Here's something you can do right now.

- Think about someone you'd love to see coming through your doorway, someone who fits your Ideal Client category. Write down some of the reasons that you enjoy, or would enjoy, working with this kind of person.

- Try thinking about this person in a more thorough way, to discover more about who he or she is. Here are a few questions to get you started:

    - What really matters to this person? Family, wealth, friends, appearances, recognition? Better health? Less pain? Time off? Getting well? Having a knee replacement? Having more children? Getting some rest? Being able to play guitar again? Getting a fresh start? Having more fun? Losing weight? Being more flexible or less stressed? Going back to dance class? Having greater involvement in the community? Finding more friends? Developing greater awareness?
    - What do you know about this person occupationally, spiritually, or otherwise?
    - Are you aware of specific interests they may have?
    - What do they do for fun, or to take care of themselves?
    - Which social media platforms do they use?
    - What kinds of social events do they attend?
    - Are they affiliated with specific groups, either online or offline?
    - What worries them, keeps them up at night?
    - What inspires them? What do they value?
    - What do you think they say to a close friend when they talk about their most pressing problems?

- Watch as a picture of your Ideal Client begins to emerge. There's some magic at work here. Through the power of your intention and imagination, you're engaging your Life Force as you move toward greater prosperity.

- Celebrate every victory! Celebrate having an idea regarding who your Ideal Client may be – even if you haven't fully decided yet.

Compose

People have little interest in
purchasing a bed.
What they want is a good night's sleep.

from the annals of marketing folklore

Compose

Step 5
Compose Your Compelling Stories

In his best-selling book *Tribes: We Need You to Lead Us*, bestselling author Seth Godin says that marketing is "telling stories that spread." The phrase 'going viral' entered our collective lexicon in the past decade, graphically demonstrating what it looks like when a story spreads.

Stories that go viral are those that inspire massive levels of interest. Some are stories told in a mostly visual form – such as a super-cute photo of a baby dancing or a hilarious cat video. They may be brief accounts, in words, of events we find irresistible: a Facebook post about a good deed performed, a life saved or the unlikely victory of an underdog.

We may not all have stories that go viral, but we can all tell stories that will reach out to our communities and prospective clients. The purpose of this is to notify the people who are looking for us about who we are, how we can help and where they can find us!

In the exciting next step in your journey to prosperity, "Compose Your Compelling Stories," you might begin thinking of yourself as more of a storyteller than a marketer. I'll show you how to write the stories that matter most and share good storytelling tips to make it easier. Your stories will be tailor-made to perk up the ears of your Ideal Client!

Because you've learned so much about your Ideal Client in the previous chapter, you already have the raw materials you need. Your prospective clients' problems will become the framework for everything you say. When you write or speak about your work, they will listen to you.

You'll learn to tell several kinds of stories, written in a way that feels authentic and honest. Your ideas about marketing will be challenged, again, in a comforting way.

You'll see that learning to communicate in a comfortable and relaxed way about what you can do to help others is not just about promoting yourself. It's also a part of your service in the world.

Let's revisit our definition of marketing.

In the very beginning of our book, I shared my definition with you: Marketing is a well-conceived and highly organized way of notifying the world about what you have to offer and how you can solve their problems. Let's go into more detail.

Marketing is made up of stories you compose to attract and retain clients and become more visible in the world. This process includes everything from the language you put on a website or brochure, to how you carry yourself, and the conversations you have with potential clients. It's how you respond to people at a networking event or in a podcast interview, how you portray your work to your peers and current clients, the business name you choose, how you conduct new client intake interviews, and so much more. Taken as a whole, all of this tells a story.

To build a prosperous business, part of your job is to take charge of your story. Doing so requires mindfulness, Vision, self-appreciation, attention to detail, and deep knowledge of your Ideal Client.

A note about language: I'll sometimes refer to your stories as 'marketing language,' my version of an industry term ('marketing copy') that applies to the words you use on your websites, brochures, e-books, email messages, social media posts, and more.

Where do these words, this 'marketing language,' come from? They come from what you know about your Ideal Client.

What kinds of stories will you need to support your marketing efforts?

You'll need more than one version of your story – in basic terms: an elevator speech, a one-minute conversation, and a series of leading questions. You'll also want a business name and a biographical story. You will tweak these stories from time to time for different occasions. However, for the most part, once you have an elevator speech, a one-minute conversation, a business name, leading questions, and a biographical story about yourself -- you'll be off and running.

P.S. As a reminder, when you see this symbol, it means this is something that we at Life Force Marketing can help you with.

Your Elevator Speech

'Elevator speech' is a fancy term for the words you use when you meet someone who asks, "What do you do?" and you only have time for a sentence or two. In some ways your elevator speech is the most difficult story to compose because it allows very little time for conveying who you are, who you serve, and the problems you solve. That sounds like a tall order, and it is! However, because you've done your initial work in Step 4, choosing the people you want to serve and how you can help them, you're ready to start. As you read the examples below, notice that in every case you get a clear sense of what this person does for a living and how they help people. A good elevator speech is dense and rich in both detail and meaning. Please notice that, in these examples, no one is talking about their modalities or art forms. *More later on that...*

The formula for a memorable elevator speech includes two components:

1. The 'I AM' statement
2. The 'WHO do I serve, and WHAT PROBLEM am I solving' statement

---

Look at the two sets of elevator speech examples below and look for the two components, either directly stated or implied, in each.

Examples of elevator speeches from TadHargrave.com and other online sources.

- The Urban Farmer works with environmentally conscious homeowners and community groups...who have the desire to live more sustainably in their own backyards but are overwhelmed by a lack of knowledge, skills, or time to achieve this on their own.
- I am a massage therapist specializing in breast massage. I work with women who have...concerns about their breast health - maybe they're having discomfort while pregnant, tenderness from breastfeeding, ... menopause, or ... breast reduction/augmentation ...

- I'm Helen, a chiropractor who helps construction workers get back to work after surgeries and accidents.
- I'm A.J., and I work with assisted living facility administrators who are feeling frustrated with their same-old lackluster programming and wanting to find uplifting, stimulating and enjoyable new activities they can offer to their residents.

Additional elevator speeches written by my coaching clients:

- I'm Lebanon, a Shamanic Bodyworker and energy worker. I help women who have lived with sexual assault regain their self-confidence, establish clear boundaries that make them feel safe, and stop blaming themselves for the past.
- I'm Linda, a Holistic Health Advisor, and I help older women who are entering a new career late in Life to move past their confusion around food and exercise, change past destructive habits into healthy new habits, and regain confidence in their bodies and their futures.
- I'm Melody, a Health Coach, and I help men and women who are preparing for major surgery by advising them on holistic supplements, teas, medicinal foods and meditation techniques so that they feel stronger, less fearful, and better prepared for surgery with the quickest possible recoveries.
- I'm Katie, a holistic vocal coach; I work with political and environmental activists who long to be listened to, to be capable and persuasive spokespeople on the subjects that matter deeply to them.
- I am Leslie, an acupuncturist, and I help caregivers who are always caring for others reclaim time for themselves and to overcome sadness and exhaustion.
- I'm Karen, a Pure Romance representative, and I help women of all ages be more playful in the bedroom and let go of some of their personal inhibitions.

Your One-Minute Conversation

Your one-minute conversation is a more extended, more conversational version of your elevator speech. You rarely deliver it in its entirety; more often parts of it are woven into discussions with others. It comes in handy at a networking event when you've already started a conversation with your elevator speech and the person you're talking to wants to know more. It comes in handy when you're having a conversation with a potential joint venture partner. It's useful when you meet a friend on the street, and he asks, "So, what are you up to these days?" It's the basic currency of speaking at a lead generation group meeting where your job is to tell others what you do and who you serve so they can refer people to you.

While you can't (and shouldn't!) genuinely plan every conversation, the point of having a one-minute conversation is to keep top-of-mind some of the main things you hope to get across when the opportunity presents itself. The focus of the one-minute conversation is still primarily on the needs and interests of your prospective clients.

A One-Minute Conversation Has Three Parts.

1. An ELEVATOR SPEECH in the beginning
2. A 'NEEDS' Statement in the middle section. This consists of 2-5 sentences which speak in detail about the problems and pain your clients are experiencing.
3. A 'HOW I CAN HELP' Statement to conclude.

Consider three examples of One-Minute Conversations from my client files. You can see why I'm very proud of the people I have the privilege of coaching.

Carol's One-Minute Conversation, in 3 parts

Elevator Speech
I am a certified health and wellness coach who helps women who are discouraged, overwhelmed, and drowning in fatigue find more energy and begin living a fuller life again.

Needs Statement
The woman I work with is frustrated because what she's done in the past to feel energized and happy is no longer working. She lacks the focus she needs to address her goals. She runs out of energy before she runs out of tasks. She struggles with self-doubt because of this discrepancy between where she wants to go and the amount of power she has available for getting there. She's afraid her circumstances won't improve.

How I Can Help Statement
We work together to identify what has been slowing her down, how diet and exercise are contributing. We look at the medications and supplements she's taking, the way she organizes her time, and the things she does for fun. Together we identify where she is and where she wants to go – her Vision -- and formulate a step by step plan to turn her Life energy around so she can pursue her most cherished goals.

Franki's One-Minute Conversation, in 3 parts

Elevator Speech
I am launching a new private practice in Lexington as a holistic health advisor. I work with people who are planning surgery and are concerned that their bodies and minds aren't adequately prepared to go through the ordeal and then heal quickly.

Needs Statement
Many of my clients have had frightening and slow recoveries in the past. Some don't trust doctors and are terrified of hospitals. They don't know how to prepare their bodies to recover quickly. They long to have a guide and advocate who will walk beside them on their surgical healing journey.

How I Can Help Statement
I provide holistic support to help them get ready, be less stressed out about what's coming up, and to heal more quickly. I can help people prepare so that they feel more comfortable and relaxed about the procedures they're facing. Using my background in therapeutic foods, I show them how to prepare their bodies nutritionally in advance of the surgery to ramp up their healing powers. I teach people about botanicals (herbs) to fine tune their healing mechanisms. I share meditation and other relaxation strategies and begin preparing them for the morning they walk into the hospital, and the day they walk out.

Shoshana's One-Minute Conversation, in 3 parts

Elevator Speech
I am a digestive health specialist working with cancer patients who are coming off of long bouts of chemo and radiation and are trying to feel good again for the first time in a very long time.

Needs Statement
My clients have difficulty eating and keeping their food down and so they feel depleted. Often, they can't taste their food, and that affects their appetites. They long to feel self-confident and optimistic again about their health and their future.

How I Can Help Statement
I help my clients learn about which foods to eat that will restore the flora of their digestive tract and a return of their appetites -- also bringing back a healthy glow to their skin. I share foods, teas, and botanicals with them that work safely with their medications. I share inspiring resources, stories, music and readings with them that help them feel their feet on the ground and regain their optimism.

Your Leading Questions

Your Leading Questions come from your Needs Statements

Leading Questions are what you use in your marketing language to get the attention of your prospective clients. These questions are carefully chosen to honestly meet your prospective clients right at their point of pain and need. You ask or draw from these questions in composing your ads, brochures, e-books, workshop titles, headlines, etc.

Does that sound mean or manipulative? I assure you it is not. As you know, most of us are being bombarded with information and advertising at a ruthless pace everywhere we go.

How can we hope to spark a meaningful conversation with a prospective client, even if we know we could help with a serious problem they have, when they're drowning in irrelevant, repetitive, over-hyped propaganda?

Thoughtfully designed leading questions are a way to stand out in the mayhem.

Everyone is looking for an answer to his or her problems. If we can provide the solutions they're looking for, we must be smart about capturing their attention. Doing so is a high service to perform for others.

Let's refer back to the one-minute conversation examples again, focusing now on the middle sections, the Needs Statements. Rather than explaining it, I'll let you see for yourself how a Needs Statement can turn into a series of Leading Questions.

Carol's Leading Questions

Needs Statement
The woman I work with is frustrated because what she's done in the past to feel energized and happy is no longer working. She lacks the focus she needs to address her goals. She runs out of energy before she runs out of tasks. She has self-doubt because of this discrepancy between where she wants to go and the amount of personal power she has available for getting there. She sometimes feels that nothing can get better.

Leading Questions
Are you frustrated because everything that worked for you in the past to stay energized and be productive no longer works for you? Do you struggle to stay focused? Do you run out of energy before you run out of tasks? Are doubts about your available power discouraging you from pursuing your dreams?

Shoshana's Leading Questions

Elevator Speech and Needs Statement combined
I'm a digestive health specialist working with cancer patients who are coming off of long bouts of chemo and radiation, trying to feel good again for the first time in a long while. My clients have difficulty eating and keeping their food down, and so they feel depleted. Often, they no longer taste the food they eat, and that affects their appetites. They long to feel self-confident and optimistic again about their health and future.

Leading Questions
Are you finally coming out of the fog of your fight with cancer and longing to taste food again? Do you still have difficulty eating and keeping your food down? Are you often depleted of the vital energy you need to plan your day? Are you longing for someone to help you find your way back to optimism about your health and your future?

On the left you'll see an example of how we used Shoshana's Leading Questions to compose a cover page for her brochure.

We could also use these questions on her website, Facebook posts, as a title for her signature talk, or as chapter titles in an e-book, among other applications.

* Thanks to Brooke Lark, from unsplash.com, for the use of her beautiful photograph in this design.

Your Business Name

Your business name is a mini-story about you and your business that you'll share with other people thousands of times in many different ways. That makes it extremely valuable as marketing language.

Often the first time we think about what we should name our business takes place when we decide to order our first business card or purchase a domain name. Many practitioners choose business names that are clever, or lovely-sounding, but don't say anything about the services their business provides. Choosing their business name is often the first business decision they make, and it's not always a smart one.

Jay Conrad Levinson, author of *Guerilla Marketing: Easy and Inexpensive Strategies for Making Big Profits from Your Small Business,* writes:

> "Guerillas are careful not to make a major error with their first business decision: the name of their business... Great names are like tiny poems; each letter, word unit, and sound should work with the others to deliver strategic messages. The right name can be the cornerstone of a lasting customer relationship...an ultra-powerful marketing (tool)."

I've noticed that, in general, holistic practitioners choose business names that have personal meaning to them, even if those names come from the over-used lexicon of wellness terminology. Consider the word "wellness" itself. A Google search shows that word appearing in 44,800,000 results. And, yet, new businesses still sprout up with the word "wellness" in their business names.

Levinson spells out why this is probably a mistake: "In a cluttered marketing environment, names that simply fit in with the rest are lost and very easy to ignore. Your name must stand apart from the competition."

At the same time, your name should give a clear hint as to the nature of your work.

Perhaps another personal story will be illuminating:

REVELATIONS: Kentucky Body Works Doesn't Work

At the time, in 1992, the word 'bodyworker' was just emerging to describe an expanding array of different massage and other healing modalities. I was drawn to that new term and decided to use it rather than the more recognizable name, 'massage therapist,' in my promotions. For my first company, I chose the name Kentucky Body Works. I was very pleased with this name!

I had a thriving massage business in those early years, thanks to the curiosity and generosity of my friends and community. However, after the telephone directory listed my name, I realized my error. The people who called from the Yellow Pages found me under the heading "Massage Therapeutic" and so they knew I was a massage therapist. That generated a lot of phone calls of the appropriate kind. However, other people ran across my name in the White Pages and elsewhere. When I received phone calls from these people, inevitably they were looking for someone to do bodywork repairs on their automobiles!

When I handed someone my business card, they often remarked with a question in their voice, "I thought you were a massage therapist?" Ha! Hilarious, right? Okay, live and learn. That's the reason I have a book to write!

Bluebird Massage

K. Erin Mills is a Lexington, Kentucky massage therapist whose Ideal Clients are elderly women in assisted living and retirement homes who need attention, companionship and gentle care. She is also one of my coaching clients.

When Erin decided to call her company 'Bluebird Massage,' she made a choice that lets us know what services she provides.

What if she had, instead, chosen to call herself Bluebird Wellness or Elder Wellness Services? We'd be left wondering, does she provide bath and body products, or mental health counseling? Is she a bodyworker of some kind or does she manage corporate wellness programs for companies who serve older people?

'Bluebird Massage' is both poetic, memorable, short, visual and communicative. Her Ideal Clients will relate well to the beautiful, simple image of a bluebird, making them prone to like Erin before they even meet her.

What a great first business decision she made.

Your prospective client's point of view is the framework for everything you talk about throughout your marketing process, from beginning to end.

Now you see why I asked you to give up your membership in the "My Work is Good for Everyone Club." It isn't possible to create a message based on the particular problems and pain of EVERYONE!

When it's time to create a website, brochure, Facebook page, poster, business card or newsletter, everything you say and every image you use will, ideally, speak to the kind of person you're trying to attract, to your Ideal Client.

> "The more that people feel you are speaking right to them, and nobody else, the more likely they are to buy. You want them saying, 'that's me! not "so what.'"
>
> Tad Hargrave

Your Bio Statement: A Story About You

How do you feel when you meet a new person, and he says, "Tell me about yourself"? If you're a serious professional listener, you may find it difficult to put on the hat of the speaker and talk about yourself instead. You may be shy when talking to a stranger about your Life, or you may be perfectly confident but unsure what to say or where to begin.

When you answer, are you more likely to say something about your personal life or your work? Do you usually feel that you fully represent yourself with your answer or do you more often come away thinking, "I should have said something else, something more interesting or memorable?"

In the course of spreading your stories, there will be times when you need to introduce yourself and talk less about what you do for others and more about who you are. These circumstances may include: your website About Us page, your press kit, your introduction to a live audience, and more. For most of your communication, the narratives about who you serve are more important than your bio info. However, your bio is a valuable piece of language to have in your pocket for when you need it. Sometimes your bio statement is what opens new doors for you.

Susan Harrow, a media coach and marketing strategist from Larkspur, California, wrote one of the most memorable bio statements I've ever read, and I often reflect on it as I help others break out of pedantic-sounding, predictable self-introductions.

> Susan Harrow is a top media coach, consultant and marketing expert whose clients include everyone from rock stars to the CEOs of Fortune 500 companies, as well as entrepreneurs, coaches, consultants, speakers, and authors.
>
> For the past 23 years, she's helped clients and seminar participants shine as guests on CBS' 60 Minutes, Oprah, Good Morning America, The Today Show, Fox News, Bill O'Reilly, Larry King Live, The Food Network, etc.
>
> You may know her as the 'Go-To Girl' for getting on Oprah. But what you probably don't know is that she was almost sold into slavery to a Bedouin Sheik in Israel for 10 camels and a mule.
>
> With her guidance, dozens of people who work with her privately and in courses, have consistently succeeded in doubling or tripling their income with PR (and sometimes even without!) by using sound bites effectively.
>
> She also designs pre-publicity programs and strategies to prepare clients for media interviews. If they don't yet have a website, traffic, products or a platform she shows them how to get those too.
>
> Susan Harrow, *Sell Yourself without Selling Your Soul*

Wouldn't you love to meet her? How could you write about yourself in a similar way that's informative, memorable and impressive?

One place to check for ideas is your Resource List! There may be something exciting hiding there that, when folded into a bio statement, will further amplify the story of who you are. You can also ask yourself questions to begin gathering the facts.

- What kinds of education have you completed?
- Where did you go to school?
- What distinguished your school or training?
- How long have you been doing what you do now?

- What kinds of clients have you been able to help in the past?
- What are your areas of exceptionality?
- What do your clients or peers say about you? (Past testimonials can be helpful.)
- Is there an accomplishment you wish was more widely recognized?
- Have you received any awards or accolades or won a contest?
- Have you ever appeared in the news? If so, what was the story and publication?

Additionally, ask yourself questions that are less related to business:

- What travel and other adventures have you had? Do you have hobbies?
- Were you ever involved in sports, dance, music, or science activities?
- Have you been part of a thought-provoking volunteer project?
- In what ways have you exercised your leadership skills?
- Are you fluent in more than one language or in an art form?
- Are you a parent, grandparent or foster parent?
- What do your friends say about you when they introduce you to someone?
- Is there something about you that most people don't know?

Bio Statement Tip: Make it sound like a story about you rather than the recapitulation of a resumé

Is there something you can include from your list that tells more about you as a person rather than focusing exclusively on your credentials?

Is there something you would like to include that will make your story more memorable -- an anecdote of some kind, for instance?

When you talk about yourself, avoid sounding like it's your resumé talking.

Bio Statement Tip: Tell your story as if introducing someone else.

If it were your job to introduce a friend to a group of peers at a conference, you would speak about them in complimentary terms, right? You would share your favorite relevant facts about them. You might throw in a personal anecdote or two. You would try your very best to make them look and sound good!

I suggest you try doing that for yourself! As an experiment, take the point of view of someone, a good friend perhaps, who knows you're marvelous and is about to introduce you as the featured speaker at a monthly business luncheon. During this experiment, rather than starting your sentences with 'I,' instead, start with 'She.' That will give you a new sense of freedom in writing and saying positive things about yourself! Here are a few questions you can ask yourself to get started:

Ask: "Why is my friend particularly qualified to speak to this group on this topic?"
Ask: "What would the members of this group like to know about my friend?"
Ask: "What will people learn from listening to my friend's talk?"

Don't be shy! Dive right in and start saying flattering things about yourself! Shower yourself with compliments!

Writing a story about yourself is an art form more than a science. I find these stories come together after hashing over the potential ingredients for a while.

I often refer back to the formula Susan Harrow used in her unforgettable bio statement about almost being sold into slavery for ten camels and a mule. Susan's a publicity expert, so it's worth deconstructing her bio statement. As an exercise, I'll apply it to a bio statement for me. (Obviously I know the most about me, so that will make it easier to give you an example. Plus, in the meantime, I get to tell you all about ME. ☺) I'm sure this will stimulate some ideas about your own bio statement.

1. Susan Harrow is a top media coach, consultant and marketing expert whose clients include everyone from rock stars to the CEOs of Fortune 500 companies, as well as entrepreneurs, coaches, consultants, speakers, and authors.

> Her introductory sentence tells what she does, highlights her most impressive accomplishments, and tells us who she works with. My example:
>
> Meriah Kruse is a top wellness professional and prosperity marketing coach for wellness practitioners, creative service providers and retirees starting new businesses. Her clients have included everyone from opera singers to entrepreneurs, acupuncturists to social workers, also network marketers, dancers, musicians, meditators, and people living with disabilities.

2. For the past 23 years, she's helped clients and seminar participants shine as guests on CBS' 60 Minutes, Oprah, Good Morning America, The Today Show, Fox News, Bill O'Reilly, Larry King Live, The Food Network, etc.

> Her second section gives us more detail, lets us know how long she's been doing this work and adds color to her narrative. My example:
>
> In the past 35 years, she's founded or operated 16 different for-profit and non-profit companies and initiatives. She's performed the roles of a marketing department, development team, public relations firm, brand manager, social media expert, event planner, booking agent, writer, graphic designer, and VP for media relations.

3. You may know her as the 'Go-To Girl' for getting on Oprah. But what you probably don't know is that she was almost sold into slavery to a Bedouin Sheik in Israel for 10 camels and a mule.

> This section tells us more about Susan, continuing to build her credibility. She provides contrast and shows us her personality with a funny story. My example:

You may know her as a former dancer and massage therapist, but you probably don't know that she once traveled to Kiev and advised the leaders of a Ukrainian industrial concern on the art of evaluating competition and forming joint ventures with American manufacturers.

4. With her guidance, dozens of people who work with her privately and in courses, have consistently succeeded in doubling or tripling their income with PR (and sometimes even without!) by using sound bites effectively.

In the fourth section, she gets specific and tells us about her successful work with clients. My example:

With her guidance, her marketing clients, especially those who don't like selling, have plowed through doubt, overwhelm and confusion to become savvy advocates for their growing holistic and creative businesses.

5. She also designs pre-publicity programs and strategies to prepare clients for media interviews. If they don't yet have a website, traffic, products or a platform she shows them how to get those too.

In the final piece of this bio statement, Susan tells us more about the details of her services, reminding us of several reasons we might seek out her help. My example:

As a prosperity marketing coach, Meriah's focus is on empowering her clients to have lucrative, gratifying, self-sustaining businesses by using both time-honored staples and cutting-edge approaches to holistic marketing.

Quirky additions: What you probably don't know is...

One of the things I did in working on the above bio idea was to make a list of quirky things from my past I thought I might use in a bio statement in the 3rd section "But what you probably don't know is..."

In doing this, I came up with a couple more versions of my bio that I use from time to time. Why don't you try doing that, too? Here's one more version:

My current professional incarnation is as the Founder, author, and prosperity marketing coach for a young company called Life Force Marketing; but, like you, there have been many adventures and reinventions along the way.

For instance, you may know me as the Founder of Gentle Adventure Retreats where I led groups of women (and sometimes men) on eco-adventures in Mexico, Hawaii and S. Carolina. However, you probably don't know that I once participated in an entirely different form of travel: camping for weeks in a field outside London, England with a thousand devotees of a guru from India.

If we know each other from a different era, you may think of me as a long-time dancer, teacher and choreographer, and Founder of the Woodland Dance Festival. Still, you may not know that, as a Silver Executive for ASEA Cellular Health, I influenced over a thousand people in starting their own businesses and helped coach dozens to higher levels of success.

If we've crossed paths in the past twenty years, you probably know me as a therapeutic bodyworker and movement educator, but there's every chance you didn't know I once taught African dance to children in wheelchairs.

I hope you can have fun with YOUR bio statement, think of it playfully so you can communicate not only the facts of your Life but also the spirit of yourself as a person.

Of course, you always want to adapt your bio statement for a specific audience. In some cases, more formality is called for, but more often (unless you're applying for employment), adding some spice to your story will make it more memorable.

Life Force Marketing is developing a course (tentatively entitled): "Writing a Dynamic Story about the Real You that Makes Your Prospective Clients Pick up the Phone and Dial Your Number." It will be available soon.

In the meantime, print out a worksheet we've designed to help you develop a biographical statement. Visit our site: www.LifeForceMarketing.com/MORE

More Good Storytelling Tips...

Good Storytelling Tip: Seek to understand before trying to be understood

A common misconception is that, when someone asks about what you do, she wants to hear all about you and your modalities. Many of us mistakenly assume she wants to know about our particular approach, specialized equipment, who we studied with, what credentials we've accumulated, etc. It's true that at some point in your conversations she will want to know about You, but that's not until you've established that what you have to say is of value to her. Until you've done that, she doesn't really care who you are and will only be half listening.

Of course, there comes a time when you share your experience, your unique approach, your superior equipment, and the other features of your business with your prospective client. However, that comes after you establish that you understand her problem and the inconvenience or frustration or sadness, etc. that's troubling her. When the time comes for you to tell her about what you have to offer, you'll be prepared to explain it in terms that are relevant to her. Because you've listened to her thoroughly, and have inquired to understand her, you'll be able to tailor your remarks to her specifically. As a result, she'll be interested in hearing what you have to say. You won't feel like you're 'selling' or pushing her or wasting her time. More than likely, you'll feel like you're offering her needed information on a subject of great interest.

Good Storytelling Tip: Use the same words your Ideal Client uses

In your marketing language, use the same kinds of words and expressions your Ideal Client might use. It's imperative that you don't use high-falutin' language or professional jargon if you can avoid it. Of course, if your Ideal Client is science-oriented or fascinated with 'tech,' you'll need to use professional jargon for them to take you seriously, but still begin by understanding their problems and perspective first.

By the way, I'm not in any way suggesting that you 'talk down' to anyone. I am suggesting that you try to speak to, and write for, people in the language that they would use themselves. Listen to your current clients and pay close attention to how they describe their problems, the pain they have associated with them, and what they say about how it feels when they get some relief. Your clients are your greatest teachers!

REVELATIONS: Learning to avoid jargon and insider lingo

I have several clients who have been coming to see me on a regular basis for lessons in the Feldenkrais Method for almost eight years. One of them is Susan. She has taught me volumes about how to use 'normal people language' in communicating about the Feldenkrais Method of Movement Education. She has done this by, on countless occasions, listening to my jargon-filled sentences, and restating the same ideas using her own words and expressions. Susan is brilliant at translating Feldenkrais-ese into everyday English. It was a difficult lesson for me to learn and, at times, I still relapse!

The Feldenkrais Method is fascinating to me intellectually, partially because its foundational premises rest on an understanding of human learning and the human nervous system that's not commonly understood. I love to educate people about these premises, and especially to talk about the newest discoveries in neuroscience, as I understand them. For that reason, I've spent an embarrassing number of hours trying to explain the Feldenkrais Method to people who just wanted to know if it could help them with their back pain or posture, enable them to play the cello more gracefully, or improve their golf swing.

Susan more or less broke me of that habit so I haven't been on a long Feldenkrais harangue with a prospective client in several years now. I now reserve my use of Feldenkrais lingo to when I'm communicating with my colleagues – or with Susan and other long-time clients who know how to dive into that unique language with me.

Good Storytelling Tip: Observe how others respond to your story

When you notice that something you say or write about yourself and your work arouses interest, make a note. Sometimes the parts of your story that you like best don't seem to garner any attention when you share them with others. Other aspects that you don't find very interesting might be just what causes someone else's ears to perk up! You'll quickly begin to sense which parts of your story pique the most curiosity in your listener. Keep those parts in your narrative and build on them.

Also, make a note of any questions you are commonly asked about your practice -- questions you don't feel prepared to answer -- and formulate a juicy answer to those questions so you'll be ready the next time around.

Good Storytelling Tip: Repetition, repetition makes it easier

If you're reluctant because you have no background in business or sales or you've had difficulty in the past figuring out what to say to others about your work -- or if speaking to others without a script makes you shake like a leaf -- this storytelling stuff may seem intimidating. I want to assure you that, especially if you do the foundational work we're recommending early in your marketing process, you'll soon find yourself saying similar things again and again, in slightly different ways.

That means it's going to get easier. You won't have to think in detail about what to say every time someone asks, "What do you do?" or "Who should I refer to you?" or "Why should I attend your workshop?" With practice, your responses will be more automatically available to you when you need them.

Still, it's not about memorizing a canned set of statements that you repeat over and over like a robot. You want to be, and sound, conversational. It's about preparing in advance the basic ideas you need to express so that your brain can easily access them when you're forming language on the spot. Being prepared will allow you to devote your best attention to asking provocative, useful questions and genuinely listening to the answers of your prospective clients.

The Payoff:
How Your Story Can Lead to Client Enrollment!

Once you have asked many questions and understand what your client needs, after you share the story about your work and how it impacts the people you serve, you will have your potential client's attention.

Therefore, when the conversation shifts to the subject of the programs you offer, and the cost and terms of your programs -- you won't have to persuade, coax, insist or trick anyone into buying from you.

You're informing them, educating them, helping them solve problems, being a tour guide of useful information that applies to their problems. This is entirely different than what most people think of as 'selling.' What you're doing is supplying accurate information, making recommendations, and allowing them to make an informed decision for themselves.

Both of you will be able to tell if you're a match for each other. Neither of you will feel pushed, uncomfortable, sleazy, compromised or defensive. Isn't that what you want?

That's the beauty of holistic marketing.

In the approach to marketing described in this chapter, you've learned to offer your deep listening to people who have a problem. You're sharing with them that you understand and that you know how to help. That's why marketing is part of your job. Unless you let people know that you can help with something that truly matters to them, they may have to continue looking for assistance instead of finally getting the help they need.

As such, your marketing becomes a part of the high calling of service.

Your innate tendency to care about others is one of your most indispensable intangible resources, so this is right in your wheelhouse! You're exercising that tendency by telling your story in a way that's relevant to your listener.

You'll hear more about client enrollment in Step 6: SELECT, in the section on Complimentary Consultations.

p.s. Add "innate tendency to care about others" to your Resource List ☺

Here's something you can do right now.

Because I'm committed to giving you actions to take during all ten steps of Life Force Marketing, I include some actions here. However, it's only fair to tell you that this step can be challenging to complete on your own. Please don't feel like you're a failure if you find this step more difficult than some of the previous ones.

The process of composing compelling stories that will spread is both an art and a science. Fortunately, your intuitive abilities and any experiences you've had in writing and interviewing others will serve you well and help you get the hang of it.

To begin…

- If you have an Ideal Client in mind, make a stab at writing your first elevator speech! You can do it.
- Write a One-Minute Conversation, too. Why not? No one's judging you, and the more you fool around with these ideas, the more comfortable you'll become with them. Study the examples. Take some action!
- If you don't know yet who your Ideal Client is, write your Bio Statement instead! Guided by the Susan Harrow examples, start by making a list of funny or surprising experiences you've had.
- Celebrate every victory! Celebrate something new you learned about composing your compelling stories. Celebrate the new ideas that are starting to pop into your head about what you want to say to potential clients, referral partners and friends about what you're doing.

Good Luck!
Now may be a good time to revisit your Vision.
It can be highly motivating.

Select

I slept and dreamt that life was joy.
I awoke and saw that life was service.
I acted and, behold, service was joy.

Rabindranath Tagore

Step 6
Select Strategies to Spread Your Stories

You're sitting on a goldmine! I'm very excited for you right now because you've completed (or at least started thinking about) what I consider to be the hardest work in marketing. You have chosen the clients you want to work with. You've learned how to speak to your prospective clients in a way that shows them you're someone who may have the skills, the means, and the compassion to assist them. Now, although there's still plenty of work ahead, you merely have to decide how and where you want to share your stories. This may seem a little complicated at first, but believe me, you've already worked through the most challenging part. I hope you're feeling proud of yourself!

Fortunately, we're living in a time when there are wildly diverse ways of spreading the stories about your private practice. You may find this array of options exciting. It's more likely, though, that you're not sure where to begin. Website? Email list? YouTube video? Live event, Facebook, speaking engagements, brochures? Which is best for you?

To make it easier, in this chapter we'll do four things:

1. Encourage you to stay cool and have fun with the process;
2. Tune in to the era you're in now;
3. Explore, compare, and explain a range of possible marketing avenues;
4. Address the potential for becoming overwhelmed.

Let's get started!

Speed Dating and Making Selections

How do you feel about making decisions? Is it something you do readily and boldly, or do you tend to chew on things for a while? One thing I suspect about my peers in the arts and healing arts is that, even if we make a list of pros and cons, we are still more likely to follow our intuition when it's time to finally decide. Does this apply to you? What's your decision-making style?

For my part, until I had my son, I made very few conscious decisions, especially related to my work Life. I was what you might call 'going with the flow.' I generally made my next move in Life based on what showed up! (That's still part of me, by the way.)

I became a dancer because I met someone on a bus in Oakland who told me about a new African Dance studio opening up. I had always wanted to study African Dance, so I went straight to the new studio and, before long I was working for the owner of Everybody's Creative Arts Center -- my eventual mentor, Halifu Osumare. I had no intentions at all of leaving my high-paying job as a corporate bank secretary in San Francisco to join Halifu's fledgling non-profit in the East Bay. However, when I met her, I felt inspired to make a change, and so I did. This decision altered the course of my Life significantly.

I know that many of dearest pals have operated their lives in precisely this way.

At this juncture in our time together, what's important is for you to have enough information to make an informed decision. Of course, you can still consult your intuition, your angels, or your Tarot cards for guidance if that's the way you roll. Get out your pros and cons list if that helps. On the other hand, if saying a prayer for guidance is more your style, now's a good time to put your hands together.

It's not an impossible decision you're facing, and the selections you make today aren't irreversible! The choices you make about your marketing channels will determine the next steps you take in spreading your stories, and each selection will require effort to bring to fruition. But, still, you can try something else later if your first choices don't turn out quite like you'd hoped. You have some latitude here, so rather than freaking out about the range of possibilities, try having some fun with it instead, imagining a few of the many ways you might spread your stories to everyone's benefit.

I sometimes advise my clients to think of this process as a matchmaking game where you want to be paired with the best marketing channels to move your micro-business forward.

Have you ever heard of speed dating? In speed dating, a group of men and women (or men and men, etc.) who are looking for partners, pay a fee to go through a process designed to help each participant quickly find someone they might enjoy getting to know better. I'd say it's the predecessor of 'Swipe Left, Swipe Right.' Typically, the women sit alone at small cocktail tables spread around the room. The men rotate from table to table. Someone from the sponsoring company keeps time and notifies the men when their 3 minutes is up and it's time to stand and move to the next table. Can you imagine?? After each encounter, both parties indicate through some prearranged mechanism whether they'd like to meet again, or not.

I'm introducing you to an array of marketing channels for spreading your stories to your tribe. Your next step is to whittle down the number of avenues you focus on to 2, 3 or 4. By selecting a few marketing avenues, you can become familiar with the ins and outs of how each one works. You can become expert at your marketing. You might think of what you're doing next as speed dating, wherein you take a quick look at a lot of ideas and take note of which ones are attractive to you. Swipe left, swipe right!

Important Reminder: You're not marketing to everyone!

If you've been going through the Life Force Marketing book one step at a time -- or even if you've been skipping around -- you will have gotten the idea by now that you're not trying to attract the entire world to your practice or business endeavor! You're only trying to attract one specific type of person, your Ideal Client. That makes it much simpler to decide what to do next!

The Era You're Living In

Recently, as I was recovering from a bad bout of respiratory congestion and the accompanying exhaustion, I wanted to let my community know that I'd been sick but was recovering, and to do it in a way that wouldn't require excessive time or energy. Because I have a supportive personal following on Facebook, I wrote out a short message, including a "thank you" to the Holistic Health Advisor who helped me get through the difficulties. I posted it with a photo of myself wrapped in blankets and obviously feeling under the weather. Within a few hours, over 100 people, friends from all over the country, saw my pitiful message and responded with kind and loving remarks. By the next morning, nearly 200 people had responded. It's bad enough to be sick, but to be sick all alone is worse. I was no longer alone.

This kind of communicating has never been possible before.

REVELATIONS: A new way to broadcast

When I first started my holistic practice, a therapeutic massage practice in 1992, we were operating in a very different landscape than we work in today as micro-businesses carving out a place for ourselves. The computer was still only beginning to arrive in people's homes, and I didn't know how to use one! *The internet wasn't in widespread use. No email. No desktop publishing. The word 'software' wasn't even in the lexicon. In those days, the name of the game was direct mailing. Each organization had someone who understood the intricacies of dealing with the U.S. Post Office and its bulk mail rules. We literally had to cut and paste together our

> flyers and brochures or hire a professional graphic designer because there was no Control X and Control V, no WORD or Pages programs! We didn't have access to the array of self-marketing choices that exist today.
>
> To announce my new massage practice, I made up flyers (cut and paste, old style), drove downtown to have them printed (no home printers yet, nor fax), drove to the post office to buy stamps, spent an evening gathering the postal addresses of friends and acquaintances, writing these addresses on envelopes, and affixing the stamps. Finally, I made yet another trip to the post office and threw my stamped, addressed envelopes in the mailbox, confident that -- in one or two more days -- friends and acquaintances would receive an announcement about my new plans in their mailboxes.
>
> Don't get me wrong; I'm not in any way down on the post office. And direct mail has its place. I'm merely commenting on the amount of time and effort required for these two different announcements, 26 years apart. The direct mail process ate up nearly two days, plus delivery time. Contrast that with the 15 minutes (and zero dollars) it took me to broadcast my "I am sick but getting better" message to 200 people.

*According to the Internet Society, "On October 24, 1995, the Federal Networking Council unanimously passed a resolution defining the term Internet."

In other words, you're living in a golden time for spreading your stories, and you don't have to spend a fortune to do it.

Dan Gregory, one of the premier marketing gurus in Australia, gave a speech at a convention for advertising agency pros a few years back in which he said: "Marketing has changed more in the past few years than in the past half-century."

Think of the implications! You might be in the right place at the right time. Now anyone can have a website, a Facebook following, a blog or podcast or YouTube video if they so desire. For the first time in history, the average individual has the capability to easily communicate with the masses. The word-of-mouth of yesterday has exploded into the viral communication of today. Rather than having a few people in major advertising agencies controlling the messages that seek out consumers (that's us) every day, there are now thousands of sources of those messages.

Choices are plentiful now. One result of that is now you have a lot more decisions to make.

With so many different kinds of promotional opportunities available to you, on what basis should you make the necessary accompanying decisions? Let's look at some of your options first, and then discuss how to whittle them down to a manageable number.

Potential Marketing Channels

Let's start with an overview of potential marketing approaches. Each of these can work for people like yourself. Many of these channels will be explained in some detail later in this chapter and in Step 7: BUILD.

To get you started, I've created several lists of marketing channels (ways to promote yourself), divided into categories:

Paid Marketing Channels
Internet Marketing Channels
National Marketing Channels
Local Marketing Channels

Paid Marketing Channels

- Google or Facebook advertising (can be local or national in reach)
- Billboards, both print and electronic
- Display ads in newspapers or magazines
- Direct mail campaigns (local and national)
- Strategically placed posters and flyers (local)
- Exhibiting (local, regional or national)

Internet-Based Marketing Channels

- Your website and/or blog
- Facebook pages, groups and events
- Linked In profile and groups
- Guest blogging (contributing your article to someone else's blog)
- Social media such as Instagram and Daocloud
- Affiliate programs
- YouTube videos
- Guest appearances on someone else's podcast
- Creating your own podcast
- Joint ventures and other forms of alliances
- Email lists, coupled with strategies for expanding your lists, for either local or national use.

National Marketing Channels

- Press releases to national media (a publicist can help)
- All internet-based approaches
- Appearing on someone else's podcast
- Appearances on major media talk shows on TV or radio

Local Marketing Channels

- Press releases to newspapers, magazines, TV, and radio
- Networking functions
- Free speaking engagements, exhibits and/or networking at:
  - health food stores and wellness centers
  - trade shows or conferences
  - fitness centers
  - churches or neighborhood associations
  - professional organizations
  - women's centers and parks departments
- Self-produced workshops on your hottest topic
- Locally oriented social media sites
- Selective alliances
- Referral programs
- Open House or Grand Opening (for either a home-based business or a 'brick and mortar' one.)
- Strategies for building your local mailing list

Next, we've compared nine different marketing channels. Most are spelled out in greater detail in this chapter or in Step 7: BUILD.

Comparing Channels for Promoting Your Business

Marketing Channel	Benefits, Advantages, and Other Notes
Press releases	Get the word out to newspapers, magazines, TV, and radio about your business. The effects are short-term and centered around an event or newsworthy development such as a new location, new services or partners. Can help you reach new people.
Networking functions	Requires little preparation once you have your marketing language and business cards. Often free of charge. Once you hone your networking skills, you'll feel confident talking about your business to anyone.
Speaking engagements	Online speaking, such as podcasts, helps build a broader audience. At in-person events, you can sell your books, or give away small gifts in exchange for email addresses.
Self-produced workshops and Open Houses	Generate income via workshops, providing cash flow. Helps build your audience for private work. Can increase word of mouth, help build your brand, garner publicity.
Website or blog	Websites continue to build your business while you're sleeping. If you do it right, you can also build a mailing list from your website. Websites are important resources which last indefinitely but need frequent updating.
YouTube or Vimeo videos	Great way to capture people's attention. Use on your website, in social media or blog posts, and more. Can be time-consuming and/or expensive.
Email marketing programs	Building your mailing list will likely be one of your top priorities. Indispensable for building a following.
Exhibiting at health fairs, community events, conferences, business events, etc.	Requires advance expense for display equipment and visual aids -- and a design idea for making an eye-catching, portable display that shows you off to your advantage. After you've prepared once, you'll be able to use these assets repeatedly. Repeat expenses include entry fees, samples, and handouts. Exhibiting in the right places can effectively develop new connections and leads – and it can be fun.
Joint Ventures	JV partners can be valuable because they expand your audience base beyond who you might ordinarily reach.

Next: Detailed info about five specific marketing channels

I've featured * five marketing channels you might find useful. These five were chosen because they are free or nearly free; they have a shallow learning curve; they are relatively low tech; and have already worked well for thousands of businesses like yours.

Networking Events
Facebook Groups
Selective Alliances
Email Lists
Complimentary Consultations

* Those featured here aren't necessarily the best for everyone. You may also need other channels such as websites, printed brochures, and introductory videos. You'll find additional details on other options in Step 7: BUILD.

Networking Events

Networking events come in many styles. Some are small and informal, others large and highly organized. What they all have in common is that everyone at a networking event knows they are there to meet new people and make new connections.

Some people say that networking is over-rated, but I can only assume they've been attending the wrong kind of networking events. IF you are attending an event that has some of your tribe present (or persons of influence who could refer you Ideal Clients), it's anything but a waste of your time. It could be the catalyst for giving your practice a friendly boost. Of course, its efficacy also depends in part on how skillfully and genuinely you participate!

In their book *Business Coaching and Mentoring for Dummies*, Authors Marie Taylor and Steve Crabb summarize the simple skills of networking:

> "Discover how to engage with others, to actively listen and take a genuine interest in them. Ask good questions that create a dialogue instead of leaving the other person feeling she's been interviewed. Be clear about if and how you may be able to help someone and follow through on your commitments. Get clear on what you would like from each networking relationship. Become confident in talking about yourself, your business, and your aspirations."

Here's what you can expect at a typical networking event: People will either be walking around or seated at tables. They might come up to you and introduce themselves. It's a give and take, and everyone's there to spread the word about their work and make new connections. Networking is the perfect place in which to practice your listening and question-asking skills, as well as your elevator speech, one-minute conversation, and snippets of your bio statement. Bring business cards, drinking water, and your happy face. If you approach the whole affair with an open heart, you'll have a good time.

Networking Tip! Please don't go to a networking event and isolate yourself. You must get up and walk around, stick out your hand and introduce yourself. Is that difficult for you? It is for many... So, practice first! Practice with your spouse or your best friend, your children or your neighbor. Stick out your hand and say "Hi, I'm so and so. Who are you? Tell me about your business." With practice you might learn to enjoy it. ☺ But, if you really hate the idea of networking, don't select it! Swipe Left!

Facebook Groups

One of the ways to up-level your involvement on Facebook is to create a Facebook Group. This way you can post to a focused group of friends who share a common interest. Groups allow you to invite friends to gather around a virtual drinking fountain. With Groups, you can post news, testimonials, surveys, videos, photos, contests, opinions, as well as product, service and event announcements.

One advantage of Groups is they provide you with a quick way to create an online presence while you're waiting to put together a website or blog.

Things to think about: What will you call your group or page? Are you using your business name? What kinds of images and posts will you share? You can only invite people who are already your Facebook friends. Who should you invite? There are two ways to think about it:

1) Invite only your Ideal Clients. If there are many of your Ideal Clients on your Facebook friends list, focus on them in your invitations.

2) Invite everyone who you'd like to notify about your practice. Especially in the early stages of your business (if you're just starting), then getting the word out, even in a less targeted manner, can still be beneficial.

With a Facebook Group, you should plan to post several times a week. As you do so, those who have accepted your invitation will often receive a notification that you've posted. Because people can comment on your posts, you can start conversations, a useful way to spread your stories and get to know potential new clients.

To use Facebook to your maximum advantage, you might seek help from someone with experience, but at the very least you can start on your own. Jump in! Get your feet wet!

You can also learn more about Facebook and just about every other question you'll ever have about social media by visiting the website of Social Media Examiner. See the *Ways and Means* page in the back of our book for details.

Selective Alliances

If you review your Resource List, you may find you've listed the names of 'persons of influence' or people who serve the same type of Ideal Clients as you, but with non-competing services or products. You may be able to form alliances with these folks! Alliances can run the gamut from very informal to highly formalized. Informal alliances may involve co-promoting a workshop or other event, putting posters or brochures on each other's check-out counters, giving demonstrations at each other's events, attending networking events together, referring customers, etc.

A joint venture is a more formal kind of partnership, a mutually beneficial arrangement between two professionals who serve similar clients, in a non-competing way. Joint ventures are symbiotic in nature, allowing each professional to amplify what they can accomplish beyond what each could do alone. Joint ventures expose businesses to new potential clients.

Would a joint venture example be helpful? Introducing Baby Birds Boutique

This imaginary alliance is between YOU, a Bones for Life and Posture Consultant specializing in pregnant women, and another businessperson, Carolyne, who runs a maternity clothing store called Baby Birds Boutique.

The two of you meet the initial criteria for a joint venture: you serve the same clients but with non-competing services and products.

You're ready to launch a new program – "Walking Tall for New Moms" – and you'll be teaching pregnant women how to improve their posture in the late stages of their pregnancies and postpartum. Carolyne realizes that her customers will appreciate learning about your new program because so many of them are suffering from back pain and your program can help with that. She agrees to co-promote your new program to the Baby Birds Boutique constituency.

After you've agreed on the details of your arrangement, you prepare your story, and Carolyne shares it with her mailing list. If any of her people register for "Walking Tall for New Moms," Carolyne will receive a commission. As a second initiative, you might also choose to send out an announcement and a discount coupon to your mailing list about Baby Birds Boutique's upcoming sale on summer maternity cropped linen pants. If one of your followers buys a pair and turns in the coupon, you will receive a commission from Carolyne.

You've each reached out to new customers and made some income! You've both demonstrated that you understand the needs of your tribe. That's a joint venture. Doesn't that sound like fun? Joint ventures are a great way to collaborate with others on your mutual success.

Many of the masters of internet marketing with ginormous mailing lists use this kind of joint venture arrangement routinely and co-promote each other like crazy. There is no reason why you can't use a scaled down version of it for yourself!

There are as many kinds of joint ventures as there are professions. Any two businesses that have something to offer each other – and where the potential for reciprocity is genuine – can help each other in any way they desire. Most small businesses are looking for ways to increase or retain their clientele. If you approach someone professionally and have a well-developed and viable idea (or just an open mind for a good conversation), you may well receive a warm welcome.

One thing you can do right away is to begin keeping an eye out for partnerships that already exist between businesses in your community. Doing so will give you a feel for the 'lay of the land.'

For example, your bank may be offering special discounts with a restaurant or real estate company. Two or more local stores may be teaming up to co-produce a joint Sale Day. A local spa may be offering specialized workshops featuring holistic practitioners. Your grocery store may be donating a portion of their proceeds to a non-profit group (a Good Will partnership). Once you begin noticing, you'll see evidence of alliances and joint ventures more commonly than you may have expected. Staying tuned to what's already happening around you can help you spot businesses who are open to partnering with others and also stimulate the flow of new business-building ideas.

There's one more kind of alliance I'd like to suggest that's ideally suited to holistic practitioners and creative service providers: Trading sessions with other practitioners in order to build a referral network.

Trading with your peers is such a natural thing for people like us to do! Many of us enjoy working outside the cash economy by trading our services for someone else's, so you may already have a trade partner or two. However, there's another way to think about trading that you may not have tried yet.

Here's how you do it: Reach out to other holistic practitioners in your area. Offer to trade sessions with them so you can learn about each other's practices. Talk to them about the specific issues you specialize in; learn about their specialties and how they approach their work. This is a form of networking, but something you initiate yourself, one colleague at a time.

In this type of alliance, what you're looking for is a partner whose specialty is well defined and distinctly different from yours.

When you come across a potential client who would be better served by your colleague, you make a referral and let your colleague know you've done so. Perhaps your existing clients have relatives or neighbors who are the perfect clients for your trading partner. This kind of joint referral program is easy and free to set up. It can make a huge difference in building your practice as well as new professional friendships.

You can see how important it is to have a target audience in this instance. If you've done the work of defining your Ideal Client, and you've developed marketing language describing the problems you address, then it will be much easier for you to explain to other practitioners the type of clients they can send your way. Share your elevator speech! Your referral partners need an easy and accurate way to describe your work, so share your own story with them in written form.

Email Lists

Email is a time-proven and straight forward method of spreading the stories you developed in Step 5: COMPOSE. Your leading questions and needs statements, your elevator speech and bio statement – each of these will come in handy over time using email. Most modern businesses will benefit from an email list.

If you're only trying to build a small to moderate size list to keep in touch with current clients and identified prospects, and to promote local events or special promotions, your email list won't require as much work or technical expertise. However, if you want to build a national or regional presence so that you can work remotely or sell group courses nationwide – or if you want to build a larger local list –

more technical knowledge will be required. In the world of internet marketing, a well-developed, large, targeted email list is the gold standard.

If you decide to build and use an email list, there are services you can use quite inexpensively that will send messages to everyone on your list automatically, thus saving you time and improving your consistency. This function is called an 'auto-responder.' With auto-responders, you write the messages, but they are delivered automatically at the time of your choosing. It's even possible to write many messages in advance and schedule them for when you want your messages to go out. Very likely you currently receive automated email messages of this sort from someone else. Read more about growing your email list in Step 7: BUILD.

Choose a bulk email provider with a national reputation. (My two favorites are Constant Contact and Mail Chimp). They'll provide you with somewhere to store your contact information, as well as templates you can use to make beautiful professional newsletters or event announcements. They'll help you keep track of those who want to unsubscribe from your list (very important!) and also those who respond to your messages favorably. You can find contact info for my favorite companies on the *Ways and Means* pages in the back of this book.

To get the most from your email marketing efforts, you may choose to ask for help in setting up your email database, newsletters and auto-responder message campaigns. Email marketing setup and implementation is a service Life Force Marketing can provide. Look for details in the *How We Can Help: Services Provided* chapter.

Complimentary Consultations

As you will see, complimentary consultations are a bit of an art form; there's a lot you can learn to prepare yourself for doing them well. This is another area where seeking out the support of a coach or advisor will help you improve your results and bring in new clients more quickly. I've used complimentary consultations to build several of my businesses; I suggest you give serious thought to adding this to your business expansion strategy.

Sometimes called Free Consultations or Discovery Sessions, complimentary consultations have an advantage to you and your prospective clients: they provide a safe conversation wherein each of you can get to know the other. This advance 'taste test' is good for your prospects, who get to sample your offering and personality without committing financially; however, it's equally valuable for you. In the course of a well-conceived consultation you'll learn a lot about the person who's considering your services.

The purpose? First: Come to a mutual conclusion in answer to the question, "Should we work together?" Second: For you to provide something of value to the person you're meeting with, even if the two of you don't decide to work together. The design below is intended to fulfill both purposes.

Now, a brief summary of the parts of a complimentary consultation

(I modified this outline from the far more detailed lessons I learned in Bill Baren's Client Enrollment Mastery program. You'll find a link to his website on the *Ways and Means* pages in the back of our book)

- Establish rapport; make sure your guest feels comfortable and welcome
- Let her know what to expect by giving a brief preview
- Learn about your prospect's problem by asking pertinent questions
- Go deeper, asking questions to find out how this problem is affecting her daily Life. Allow her to experience the problem and its effects on her Life, a process that may be somewhat emotional for her.
- Ask how her Life would be different if this problem were solved. Encourage her to envision what she wants, where she hopes to go.
- Ask what the impact on her Life would be if she achieves what she wants.
- Ask what roadblocks or challenges are getting in her way.
- Share a mini-case study that's relevant to her obstacles. Let her know that you have experience or a solution in this area.
- Ask if your prospect is open, now, to hear about how you could help her.
- Assuming she says "Yes," explain your services and programs. Recommend the program or plan you think will help her most, that's the best fit for her.
- Ask: "Now that I've explained the program I think is the best fit for you, what do you think the benefits of going through the program would be for you?"
- Ask if she has any questions. She will probably ask you about your pricing now. It feels less pushy when she asks rather than you just telling her.
- Answer her questions and provide the pricing. Ask "Which option sounds the best to you?" or "Is this something you'd like to get started with?"

My contributing editor, Balin Kruse-Williams, has several suggestions about the conclusion of this process -- often referred to as the 'Closing.'

> "Most people think of closing as a high-pressure sales tactic used to convince someone to buy. But that's not what we do in holistic marketing. For us, closing someone simply means you're collecting a decision. You've done the work of learning about her problem, you've outlined your solution to that problem, and now it's time to simply ask her if she wants to take advantage of your solution.

You're not trying to convince her to become your client; you're not saying: 'Hey you should really do this because of x, y, z.' You're merely asking what she wants.

Here are a few more examples of closing questions:
'Does this seem like something you're interested in doing?'
'Would you like to schedule your first appointment?'

If she seems interested, but not entirely sure, she may have lingering questions about your practice. The following prompts may encourage her to ask you those questions:

'Is there anything you're unsure of that I could clarify?'
'What kind of information can I give you, that would help you decide if this is right for you?'

If she seems highly interested, you may not even have to ask a closing question.
'I have openings next week. Would you like to get started?''"

A few additional useful guidelines:

1. Your complimentary consultation is not an advertisement for your services. It's a time when you genuinely learn about your prospective clients and find a way to impart something of value to them – usually within a 30- to 60-minute time frame. Like any good conversation with a potential Ideal Client, your complimentary consultation begins by asking questions.

2. Always assume the person sitting in front of you has a need; otherwise, they wouldn't be sitting there! Ask direct questions to find out what that need is. If you don't find out what's troubling them, they probably won't be interested in your services.

3. Sometimes people are reluctant to be honest with themselves about the pain their problem is causing them, or about their history of avoidance in regard to solving it. Part of your job is to gently remind people – largely through the way the consultation is structured, as indicated in Bill Baren's outline above – that their situation isn't likely to improve unless they take new action. Although you may not be accustomed to interacting with people in this way, it's a profound service.

4. When it's time for you to talk about your services and programs, talk about what you can do for them individually; don't speak in general terms.

5. Be prepared to make a sale. In some cases, your prospects will conclude you're the person they're looking for, but they won't be ready yet. That's okay; be happy! Ask when they'd like to begin. However, just as often, they've come to see you because they're ready for help right now. Assume they're prepared to buy and speak with confident assurance. Have your program offerings written out and your calendar on hand so you can schedule their first session. Be prepared to process their payment.

6. Be prepared to show your leadership in the matter of their problem. IF you conclude this is someone you'd like to work with, be prepared to say, with conviction, "I would love to work with you. This is what I recommend..."

Strategic Thinking

Now that you have some initial exposure to a host of marketing channels, let's think strategically about selecting the best ones for you.

I'm going to borrow from someone who knows the subject like the proverbial back of his hand. Verdis Norton, Co-Founder and Board Chairman Emeritus of ASEA Cellular Health, an international biotech company based in Salt Lake City, is beloved by hundreds of thousands of ASEA associates and respected as a former advisor to top CEO's in the United States. With his son, Tyler Norton, he co-created a program that's now taught to management teams and executives around the world called "Strat-Link."

Verdis is a master in this area; he's the Strategy Guy. You wouldn't usually have a man like him whispering in your ear to help you maximize a growing holistic or creative business, but today we'll borrow his words because they're relevant and provide a framework that fits well here.

> "Strategy is nothing more than thinking about resources and competencies that you have and leveraging those -- using those -- to create a sustained advantage."
>
> Verdis Norton

One piece of advice I know Verdis would offer if he were mentoring you – it's a key concept in his strategic planning approach -- is this: "Write down all your Resources, especially those that could be leveraged in some way to create an advantage for you."

Guess what? You've already done that! The Resource list you made in Step 3 fills the bill perfectly! Now you can look at your list with a more strategic eye.

Your Resource List may be full of clues suggesting one means of promoting yourself over another.

For instance, perhaps you were a nurse in your previous work, and now you help hard-working women with busy jobs find ways of eating and exercising that fit into their lifestyles. It could be strategic for you to promote your new practice to your former nurse colleagues, who would tend to trust you. Or, maybe you're a romance consultant, and one of your resources is that you've received a lot of professional bodywork and know a good bit about the mind-body connection. You might make a strategic decision to align yourself with the wellness community. You could offer a referral bonus to massage therapists or create a joint venture.

Review your Resource List one more time. Do you see something there that would give you a strategic advantage?

Consider a few more ways your resources might lead you to select a particular marketing channel:

Your Resource List	A Strategic Marketing Choice
If you have client testimonials from earlier in your practice	They would add impact to a blog, website or brochure, thus helping to bolster your credibility.
If you're a graduate of a prestigious or well-known training program	Use credential to differentiate yourself from other people who do work similar to yours but aren't as well-trained. Especially good leverage if your Ideal Clients tend to be well-educated themselves. Send out a press release after you graduate. Refer to your training program in your promotional materials.
If you have a background in public speaking	It would make sense to use it to your advantage by looking for opportunities to speak, off- and online.
If you have a background in writing	A blog, social media campaign or e-book would come naturally to you.
If you were raised on an organic farm and your work is related to food as medicine, healthy lifestyles, etc.	You would have an advantage in doing a podcast about organic farming – something others providing similar services may not have the expertise or connections to do.
If you are a member of groups, either online or in your local community	You can contact your group members in an organized way, such as direct mailing, or by inviting members to lunch or coffee in small groups or one at a time. If you have strong relationships in these groups, you can ask a few of the members for feedback on your ideas, for opportunities to speak to the entire group, or for referrals.

Now that you've seen how a strategic assessment of your resources can impact your selection, let's look at it another way.

One question will inform every decision you make about the optimal ways to reach your prospective clients:

Will This Help Me Find The People Who Are Looking for Me?

Because you know quite a bit about your Ideal Client, you can ask intelligent questions to help you evaluate specific marketing channels:

- Is this likely to be a place where my tribe hangs out? (Facebook, Linked In, DaoCloud, wine bar, dance class, book club, health food store, writer's group, painting class, meditation group, women's club, summer camp, church, Meet-Up group, university lecture, Sierra Club hike, Sunday mass)

- Will my tribe relate well to this? (videos, blogs, podcasts, Open Houses, public speaking, text messages, one-on-one meetings, direct mail)

- Can I be particularly effective at getting my message across through this type of media or that type of event?

Potential marketing channels should be considered not only for how useful they can be alone, but also for how they might work together to enhance each other. For example:

- If you're hosting a blog, you can include a way for people to sign up for your email list from your blog page.
- If you're doing a lot of networking, you can promote your complimentary consultations when you meet new people.
- If you're forming a Facebook group, occasionally post how your followers can gain access to a free e-book that also signs them up for your mailing list.
- If you plan to exhibit, your brochure will come in handy. Likewise, if you have made a video, you may be able to show it in your exhibit space.

It's possible that your chosen marketing channels will change over time.

For instance, if you love being on camera and have some of the needed resources to organize video production, you may want to start your own YouTube channel. However, that requires a lot of upfront work, and probably expense, so you might postpone the YouTube channel until the second phase of your marketing when you've already gotten the basics in place, and income is flowing in at a steady pace.

The Possibility for Overwhelm

Allow me to remind you of something. Although you may initially see 10 or 15 workable ways of reaching out to people, you'll only select 2 - 4 of them, especially in the beginning. Unless you plan to have a marketing and promotion staff, a social media manager or publicist, or other professionals at your beck and call, you'll only be able to manage a few marketing solutions. Fortunately, if you select the right ones, and understand how to use them, that could be all you need to grow your business.

When you see charts and lists like the ones in this chapter, and again when you begin building out your selected infrastructure and putting everything in motion in the next chapter, you may sometimes feel that there's always something more you should be doing, that the work of marketing is never done. Although this feeling is understandable, it's also not at all necessary. Here's a path to feeling more relaxed about it:

Create an overall promotional plan. It will become your guide for daily, weekly, monthly and occasional activities.

Get organized with a plan for what needs to be done this week, this month, in 90 days, in 6 months. If you do so, your marketing will all begin to fall into place. Some marketing tasks only need to be done once a year, such as renewing your domain name. Others need attention 2 or 3 times a week, such as Facebook posting. If you decide to produce or participate in live events, it will involve considerable advance scheduling to get all the logistics and promotion in place.

Whatever you decide to do, I recommend you put it all in your plan. A plan is an excellent antidote to the feeling of overwhelm. When you follow your plan, you can feel satisfied that you've done what's needed! Then you can get back to the activities of your business that you love the most! After all, your Vision for the private practice or small business you want isn't all about engaging in marketing activities all day every day, is it?

You can find ideas for organizing your promotion calendar on our website. LifeForceMarketing.com/MORE

Here's something you can do right now.

Go back and review all the marketing methods I've listed in this chapter and see if any jump out at you as being a good match. Choose one of the marketing channels and begin to imagine how you could use it to reach your Ideal Clients.

- Start with familiar things. For instance, if you already have a Facebook presence, ask yourself, "How could I use Facebook in new ways to reach out to my Ideal Clients?"
- As you're reviewing these potential marketing channels, apply the all-important question: "Will this help me find the people who are looking for me?"
- Look for clues on your Resource List, searching for something that could give you a strategic advantage.
- Are there persons of influence you could find a way to meet, people who are relevant to your target audience? A group you'd like to join?
- Is one marketing channel likely to reach your Ideal Client more efficiently and effectively than the others? Is there something you're just itching to try?
- Write some things down in your marketing notebook. You'll see the evidence of your thinking a week or two from now. If you haven't written it down, some of your very best ideas may disappear forever!
- See what you can come up with by taking the first stab at it. Be open to creative ideas emerging! You may think of something that's not even on the lists!
- Celebrate every victory! Celebrate your growing understanding that you don't have to do *everything*, just a few wisely chosen things, to promote your holistic, integrative, alternative, complementary or creative practice.

Now, on to building your infrastructure!

Build

Everyone who's taken a shower has had an idea.
It's the person who gets out of the shower,
dries off and does something about it
who makes a difference.

Nolan Buhnell

Step 7
Build Your Marketing Infrastructure

I wonder how you're feeling about this journey we've been on together since you picked up our book and started reading? During the months it took to hammer out these ideas in a coherent form, I thought of you continually. I tried to imagine how you would respond to this holistic marketing approach. Naturally, I can't help but wonder how you're feeling now that it's finally time to begin doing the marketing tasks themselves.

In case you're wondering, I call this phase "Building" because it feels to me like a construction process, whether I'm making a brochure or website, a newsletter or Facebook page, a live event or email list. Granted, this is not the kind of building that uses nails, hammers, concrete, and steel beams. But, still, there's a process, and it often needs to be done in a particular order, step by step. Like a more traditional construction process, this one ends in a useful product that exists in the world, a source of pride. Soon you'll have completed your marketing channels and they'll start singing your unique song to the people you're inviting into your practice! Your stories will begin to spread.

Note: Everyone uses this book in their own way, in their own time.

You may still be reading through it for the first time; you may have done one or two exercises. You may be relentlessly reading every word, doing every exercise, filling your notebook, and creating the building blocks you'll be using to make it all happen. You may have decided to wait until you find a marketing coach to stand beside you throughout the process. Wherever you're at in this business-affirming process, feel good about it! Keep taking one more step forward every day. In the meantime...

Congratulations!! Celebrate the victory of coming this far!! Now the fun really begins. A quick recap:

- You've developed your Vision for the Life you want to live, and the business that will serve as your vocational hub.
- You've learned how to feed the stories that support your Vision by giving them your attention.
- You've assessed your resources, everything you can bring to the project of fulfilling this dream of yours.
- You've thought about who you want to serve and the problems you can help them solve.
- You've thought about the best way to communicate with your tribe in a language that's relatable.
- Perhaps you have chosen your business name, written your elevator speech and one-minute conversation, picked a few leading questions and composed a biographical story about yourself. If so, you have intelligent, well thought out, strategic marketing language to use in any way you choose.
- If you've selected the marketing channels you're going to use to spread your stories to Ideal Clients, building out your infrastructure will be oh-so-much simpler.

When many people think about 'marketing,' they assume right away "Oh, I better get myself a website and buy some business cards." Commendable! Yes, definitely commendable because taking these actions represents a bold and definitive statement to the Universe about your intentions.

However, this is also a case of getting the cart before the horse. Just think about how much better prepared you are NOW to commission a new website or design your business card. Imagine if you'd tried to do so without knowing who your Ideal Client is! How in the world would you know what to say?

Because you have made strides in identifying your niche and your Ideal Client, because you've worked on your needs statements and leading questions, you know many of the essential words to include on a website or business card. You may now have a business name that was chosen based on your knowledge of your tribe rather than because it was a name you liked. You now have an understanding of your Ideal Client that will become the basis of all your marketing efforts. You're in a position now to put the horse and the cart in the right order!

The Story of Bob the Painter

I'd like to tell you about my next-door neighbor and friend Bob Stoops. He's an accomplished and handy man. He takes excellent care of his home, garage, truck, kayaks, fences, driveway and lawn. And he's absolutely phenomenal with his grandchildren! I love this guy, and his equally productive, inventive, artistic and effervescent wife, Debbie. They are the best neighbors imaginable.

Recently, Bob and I were talking while he was up on a very tall ladder scraping paint from the upper reaches of his house. He talked about all the steps that have to come first, before he can apply the new coats of paint, and how these steps require a certain amount of patience. Scraping, replacing rotten wood, filling holes, replacing bad nails, putting down a coat of primer -- all that work comes first before a drop of the final paint color goes on.

"You know," he remarked, "The satisfying part is putting on the paint!"

So, here we are now. You've done all the preparation, and it's time to get out your best paint brush. You've chosen your colors! It's time to paint.

The next phase of your work entails learning the ins and outs, the when's and where's – and certainly the HOWs – of creating the marketing channels you've chosen. To help you as much as possible, I've divided this chapter into two sections:

- Building Your Marketing Infrastructure
- Knowing When and How to Get Professional Help

Part 1:
Building Your Marketing Infrastructure

It won't be necessary for you to acquire a detailed understanding of how to build every type of marketing channel under the Sun. Indeed, as mentioned in the book's introduction, it would take thousands of pages for me to explain, step by step, how to build every major marketing channel in existence. Taking into account our ongoing give and take between providing you the 10,000-foot view and the occasional detailed how-to information, I've decided to detail the building process for ONE channel. This process is something simple but often necessary that could be helpful -- the design, production, and distribution of a printed brochure. By walking you through this one complete process, I hope to clearly illustrate how the marketing language you've developed around your Ideal client is the foundation of all of your marketing.

I'll also provide a basic introduction to several additional commonly used marketing channels. You'll find comments on each to help you determine if it's something you can do yourself. When possible, I'll offer direction on where to go for more information. I hope this will enable you to understand what's involved in building the channels you're interested in and how the work you've already done can help with that undertaking.

Building a Brochure: The Design, Production, and Distribution of a Printed Brochure

Once you have your elevator speech, your one-minute conversation, and bio statement, then you essentially already have the words you'll need to make a brochure (and more). If writing or design isn't your forte, then consider hiring a 'copywriter' to polish up your marketing language, and a graphic designer to make the brochure look amazing. Life Force Marketing provides these services, and we'd be happy to help you. However, this is something you may be able to do on your own: try if you want to! You can find a link to websites providing free, high-resolution photos and free design software in the *Ways and Means* chapter at the end of our book.

The most straightforward formats you can choose between are bi-fold or tri-fold brochures. I like the tri-fold because it provides six different information panels for adding your words and images. If you like, one of those panels can contain your return address and serve as a mailer so that you can mail your brochure without an envelope.
I've included an example of a tri-fold brochure, both in template form and as a fully designed brochure on pages 146 and 147. Here's some background to show how my Ideal Client and leading questions informed the design.

Ideal Client:
My ideal clients are creative or holistic service providers or recent retirees going into business for themselves. They're on a mission to improve people's lives through their skills and insights. They are good at what they do but unhappy with the size of their client base. They feel they should be making more money, and they know marketing may be the key, but they either don't know much about marketing, have already tried things that didn't work out, or have never been in business before. My ideal client may have some marketing background, but more likely they don't have any real interest in the subject and may even dislike the whole idea.

Leading Questions:
Are you unhappy with the size of your clientele? Do you wish your clients could find you more easily? Do you wish someone could help you with an overall marketing strategy, or with step-by-step coaching? Is your most pressing need to get help with your design and writing?

After completing your brochure design, where will you have it printed?

Advice on Choosing a Printing Company

Here are a few guidelines for selecting a printing company you'll be happy with:

- Set up an appointment to meet them in person if possible.
- Ask to see samples of their work.
- Ask about their typical timelines (how long, for instance, would it be before they could put your brochure in production?)
- How do they like to receive source materials (email, Dropbox, pdf files, jpgs)? Are they flexible?
- Do they have different choices of paper you can consider? Do they keep a variety in stock, or is everything special order?
- Do they charge extra fees for layout or are there other hidden fees?
- Do they work with a graphic designer from whom you could get some assistance if you need that? A photographer? An illustrator?
- Do you see a proof before your piece goes to print?
- What do they charge? Do they guarantee their work?
- Can they give you the names of a few satisfied customers?

If you like the answers you receive, and you generally have a good feeling about the person, give them a try! On the other hand, if you feel some hesitancy, sense a red flag, if you don't like the quality of their work, or if they're in a hurry and don't have time to be bothered with your questions -- move on.

A personal note... I use a local printer for everything I do, Beau Graphics in Lexington, Kentucky. I'm aware that I could use an online printing service and it might sometimes be less expensive to do so. However, I have an excellent, long-time working relationship with my printer. He helps me problem solve and provides technical expertise. I can call him anytime I need help. I trust him to do excellent and timely work consistently. Under no circumstances would I trade his services for a cheap print job through a service that provides zero human contact or inferior service.

A Brochure Template: COVER page, 3 panels

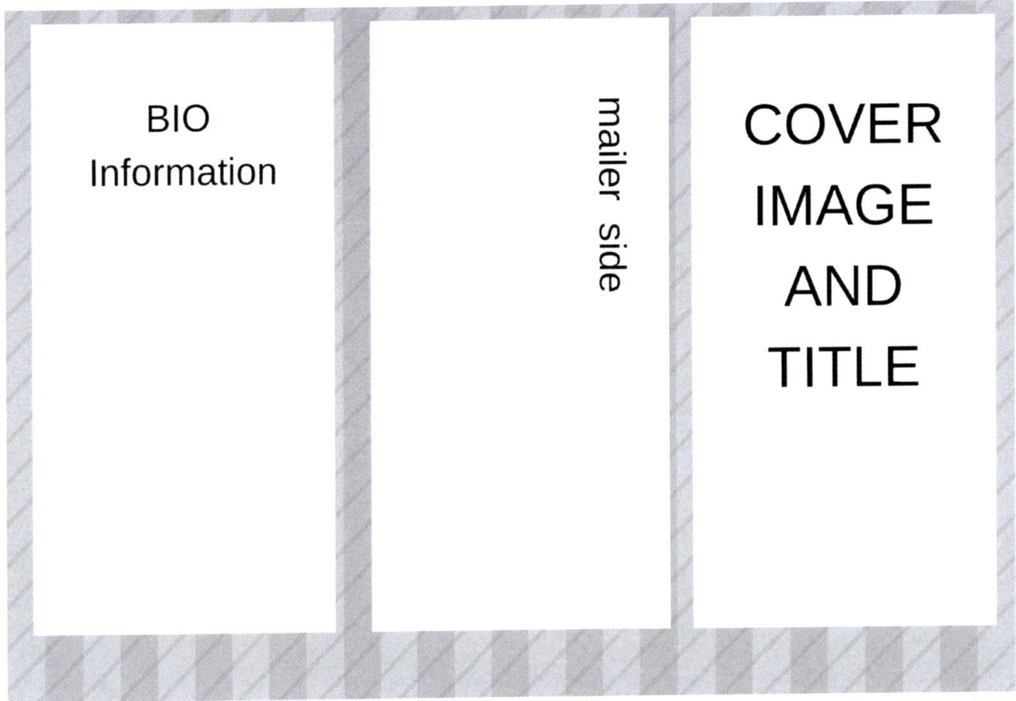

A Brochure Template: INSIDE page, 3 panels

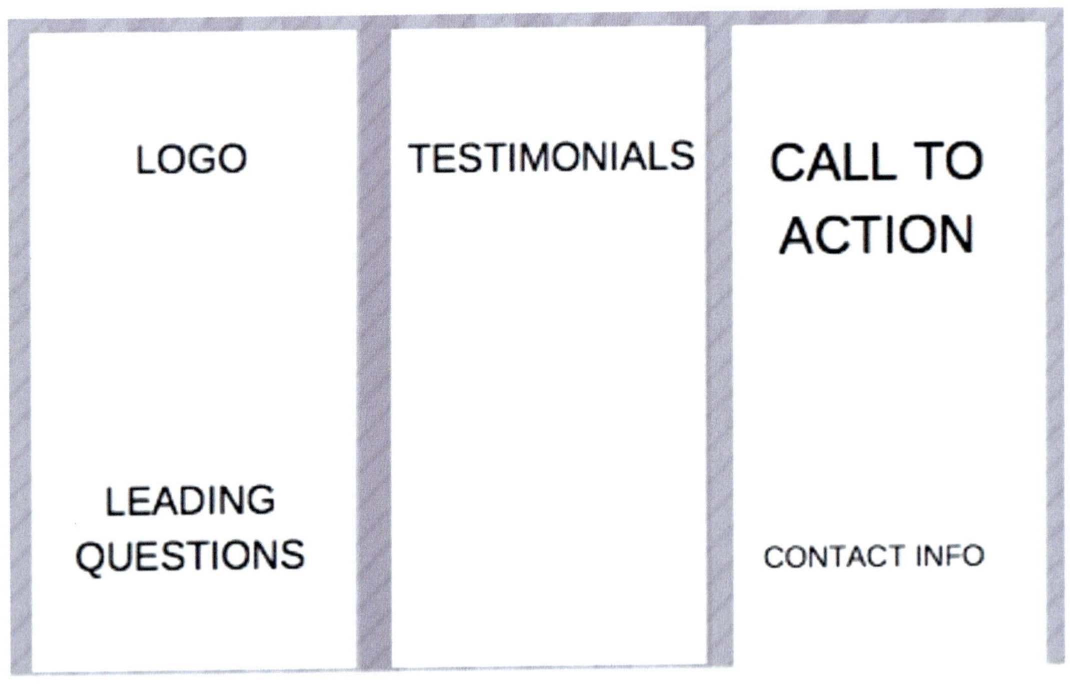

ONE SINGLE IMPORTANT MESSAGE OF YOUR CHOICE

A Completed Brochure Design: COVER page, 3 panels

A Completed Brochure Design: INSIDE page, 3 panels

After you've completed a PRINTED brochure, how can you distribute copies of it to spread your story?

Brainstorm places where you can leave a stack or mini-exhibit of your brochures. Where? That depends! You're looking for places where your tribe hangs out. Maybe you place your brochures in a:

health food store, maternity clothing store, motorcycle club, chamber of commerce, yoga studio, gym, fitness center, vitamin store, senior citizens center, produce market, coffee shop, women's center, athletic wear shop, university, church, beauty salon, library, or daycare center.

And how else can you distribute them?

- Mail a brochure to everyone on your postal mailing list
- Give your brochures out at networking events
- Use a brochure as a follow-up after you meet someone at a networking event
- Feature your brochures in your exhibit booth
- Share your brochure with each one of your selective alliance partners

Do you have some additional ideas?

One more thing:

Celebrate your new brochure! ☺

Part 2
Knowing When and How to Get Professional Help

There are some marketing channels that you won't be able to or will choose not to build yourself.

Depending on which channels you choose, and what your strengths are, you may need to hire someone to help you with some of these building projects. You could elect to seek out a coach or advisor who can walk you through specific processes step by step. On the other hand, you might decide just to hire an expert who will ultimately handle it all for you and not teach you anything! Or, you may prefer to figure it out for yourself. All of the above are perfectly legitimate options.

In Part 2, I'll discuss how to decide which things to do yourself and which tasks to outsource, including those you could outsource to Life Force Marketing. The intention is to help you get a realistic sense of what's involved in building out your marketing infrastructure. It's a creative process, often a technical process, and it can be exciting and fun. The central question on your mind right now probably is:

Should I build my marketing infrastructure myself, hire a marketing coach to show me the way and move the process along more quickly, or hire someone to do everything for me?

Unless you're multi-talented and have an incredibly versatile set of skills, you'll either need to learn a few new tasks or find someone who can complete them.

I don't want to discourage you from learning to do this building work yourself if you're so inclined. I'm a believer in life-long learning and admire anyone with a do-it-yourself inclination and the persistence to see it through. So, by all means, if you want to learn, for instance, to make your own WordPress website -- do it! I learned to do it; I've made several WordPress websites. I'm glad I have that skill set.

However, I would be remiss if I didn't tell you this:

For every new skill you decide to take on, it will slow down your progress toward your ultimate goal of having a thriving practice.

If you're not in a big hurry, that might be fine. But if you need to get on track and start bringing new clients in the door sooner rather than later, hire or trade with someone to help you.

For most people, this will be a time to find professional vendors and/or a marketing coach with specific skills. *Chapter 8: ENLIST goes into detail about the role of a marketing coach.*

Knowing whom to use can make a big difference in your happiness and your budgeting process. Having a good working relationship with each of your specialized helpers is part of building your team.

You'll find ideas for internet-based resources at the end of this book in the *Ways and Means* chapter. However, in many cases, you'll benefit more from working with local people in your area, and for this purpose I suggest you do something (not very scientific!): ASK AROUND. Getting recommendations from people you trust is the easiest way to begin your search for local helpers such as printing companies, graphic designers, videographers and video editors, photographers, and others.

Talk to friends and acquaintances who are already in business. Those who are already engaged in marketing and promotion activities, including those you do business with yourself (insurance agent, car repair guy, boutique owner), probably already use some of the very professionals you're looking for.

Because you may decide to have a website one day, because creating websites is a pretty technical affair, and because there are thousands of people offering to make your website, I'd like to provide you a bit of advice on choosing a web designer.

As with choosing a printing company, asking good questions of your prospective web design team will establish your level of discernment and send a message that you only want to work with high quality, reliable, pleasant, professional people.

Advice on Choosing a Web Designer

Whether you're shopping from scratch for a web design company or contemplating a package deal offered through your school or other institution, you'll need to ask some intelligent questions before deciding to buy. (Some of the following terms may not be familiar to you. Use Google or a tech friend to help you understand what you're asking.)

- What platform do you use: WordPress, etc.? Or do you write your own code?
- What are your fees? Do you charge a flat fee, a per-page or hourly fee?
- If a flat fee, how many pages do you include, how many images? Are videos included?
- How much do you charge to maintain the site monthly? What does that fee include? Backups? Software and plug-in updates?
- Will I be paying a hosting fee or is that included? What is the cost?
- Will my site be designed so that a novice can add text and images to update? Will you or your team be teaching me how to make the necessary changes to my site or will all changes need to be submitted to the web developers?
- If you will be teaching me how to make those changes, is doing so included in your price? How about the updates? If you're doing it for me, what is the turnaround time?
- If I need tech support do I speak to someone directly or go through email or chat? Is there a limit on how much support I can receive?
- What are the security measures included? Malware protection? SSL certificate?
- What do you provide in the way of SEO (search engine optimization)?
- What functionality does my website include (especially if a package deal): Shopping cart? Email capture? Scheduling app?

By all means, ask to be connected to satisfied customers and look at their portfolio of websites.

If you feel uncertain or sense a red flag, if they're in a hurry or seem impatient with your questions -- move on. In any case, as this may be a subject matter outside your comfort zone, don't hesitate to ask more questions, and by all means, DON'T sign on the dotted line until you're satisfied. It's okay to walk away and think about it. That's better than agreeing to work with someone before you feel confident of their integrity and good intentions.

Advice on a Few More Marketing Channels:

Your First Exhibit

If you have numerous or recurring exhibiting opportunities that cater to your Ideal Clients, I'd recommend you explore this as an option. Please read that sentence again, because exhibiting for exhibiting's sake isn't worth it, but IF you have a chance to be with your Ideal Clients on a recurring basis... go forth.

Benefits include: Meeting a lot of new people quickly, having an opportunity to collect new email addresses, meeting other exhibitors (which can lead to selective alliances), practice at telling your story in sound bites, and having a good time.

Each exhibiting venue will provide varying degrees of support. Some provide nothing but a table with a tablecloth and (if you request it) access to electricity. Others have fancier settings with built-in backdrops or other structures.

The trickiest part of setting up your first exhibit is visualizing what your booth, or space, will look like. You want an attractive display that represents you, your company and your services professionally. I recommend doing some research online; look for photos of other companies' exhibits, and imagine how you might modify those designs.

You can find exhibit design resources on our website:
LifeForceMarketing.com/MORE

To realize your design, next you'll want to procure the equipment, décor, and supplies needed to make it attractive and functional. You may wish to purchase useful items such as display stands, fabric, large signs or lettering, tripods, clipboards, acrylic or metal brochure and sign holders.

If you want to show video, you'll need to bring a computer or self-contained video monitor.

You will, of course, need things for people to browse and take home with them, such as brochures, business cards, other handouts, or small gifts.

There's an entire industry that exists to make you look good while exhibiting, and it's entirely possible to spend a lot of money going shopping with these companies. Great fun! My opinion is that you shouldn't exhibit at all unless you can look good (whatever that means to you)! On the other hand, there are many ways to do so without breaking your bank. You're a solo or very small business; it's difficult to compete visually with bankers and large real estate companies, etc. and their ten thousand-dollar exhibits. One of the best things you can do is enlist the support of a friend with a design background, or hire a designer, to help you with your overall concept and its implementation. The one thing that justifies spending money on your exhibit is that you can use most of it again and again.

Can you build this yourself? If you have a flair for design and merchandising, you can do this. However, as is always the case, if this is not one of your strengths, I recommend you ask for help because you don't want to put in a lot of time and devote financial resources and not be fully prepared to get the most out of the experience. After you have a workable, communicative and attractive design, and have all your equipment and supplies lined up, you'll be able to exhibit repeatedly without help. You can look for a specialist in this area by using search terms such as "trade show displays" and the name of your city. Other kinds of pros who could help you are interior designers, visual artists, graphic designers, and retail merchandising professionals.

Exhibiting Tip 1

Conduct a drawing for a giveaway gift. Each person who visits your booth puts his or her business card in a silver dish or small decorative basket you're provided, and you draw names for the giveaway. New email addresses! This is your primary reason for exhibiting! Now you can follow up with a note to everyone -- within two days, please.

Exhibiting Tip 2

Don't stand behind your table, stand in front of or to the side of it. You want to be available to move around and interact with passers-by.

Exhibiting Tip 3

Take care of yourself, especially during longer exhibits. Wear comfortable shoes, keep a source of protein and plenty of water on hand. Get off your feet periodically.

Exhibiting Tip 4
Ask for help. Bring someone along who can help you carry everything in from your car, set up your exhibit, and break it down at the end. Exhibiting can be demanding; don't make it worse by doing it all alone.

Exhibiting Tip 5
Have your very short pitch ready so that when people stroll by your exhibit, you can lead immediately with words that you've already thought through. What you're trying to do is start a conversation, so what you say is less like your entire elevator speech and more like a headline, a quick offer, and/or a question.

YouTube or Vimeo Videos

Videos are great places to use the stories you've composed and to spread them broadly. Slick, highly-produced video is expensive and requires professional help in scripting, storyboarding, shooting and editing. Still, don't rule that out if you have the resources! Alternatively, you can make a short video using your own story and photos, without even touching a video camera (in iMovie, for example)!

You can find a sample of a very brief 'no camera' video I made on our website: LifeForceMarketing.com/MORE

What kind of video should you make? Perhaps one that teaches a short lesson of interest to your Ideal Clients, something biographical to use on the Home Page of your website, or a short talk about the services you provide. You can post this video in literally dozens of places, including social media and blog posts. The video platform that receives the most attention is YouTube, but because it's the biggest player, it sometimes sets restrictive policies that aren't beneficial to smaller players. That's one reason that Vimeo, a YouTube alternative, is also worth a look.

Can you build this yourself? Obviously, a fancy video is for the professionals. If that's what you want, employ a video production company that provides both camera work and editing. However, to make the simpler form of 'no-camera video' I've mentioned is far easier. It still requires you to learn some form of online video editing software. I took a 2-night course in i-Movie at my local library, which was a great help. Soon thereafter I produced two videos that I'm pleased with, and it was fun doing it. If you think this all sounds doable, and you have selected video marketing as one of your marketing channels, I'm confident you can learn to do it. However, as always, if you don't want to or don't have the time – get help.

Growing your Email List 101

I said earlier that this is not a comprehensive book about internet marketing, and it isn't. However, I'd like to share just a few details about one crucial aspect that every internet marketer uses: Growing an email list. We'll discuss several of the main elements: lead magnets, landing pages with email capture, email marketing services, and auto-responder messages.

Internet marketing can be used to attract new potential clients (also called 'leads'), sell stuff, and build tribes, among other things. To do this effectively, you need to have a list of people who are interested in what you do, and you need to stay in touch with them. The more you grow your list, the more you can share your stories.

Lead Magnets. A lead magnet is one term for a free giveaway you use to entice your Ideal Clients to join your email list. The idea is to offer something interesting and valuable that you can give away completely free of charge. Your lead magnet can come in many forms: e-books, images, reports, infographics, a list of tips, a list of resources or exercises, to name a few. You can create your own, or buy something to give away.

Landing Pages for Email Capture. After you've made or purchased your lead magnet, the next thing to do is create a page to promote your giveaway -- often called a "landing page." Your landing page contains a button that says something like, "Click here to receive your free e-book." You've probably seen these many times before! When someone clicks on that button, two things will happen. She'll be asked to enter her email address, and you'll provide her access to your e-book. Because you'll now have the email address, this process is sometimes known as 'email capture.'

Email Marketing Services. I went into some detail about email marketing services in Step 6: SELECT, so you may want to refer back to that information. What I'd like to add here is that, after someone signs up for your email list by clicking on that magic button to receive your free lead magnet, you must arrange for the new email address to be stored somewhere for your future use, automatically. After all, the whole point is to build a more substantial list so that when you have something to say, you can tell it to a large group of interested parties. The two companies I've used and recommend for this job are Mail Chimp and Constant Contact.

Auto-responder Messages.
As we discussed in Step 6: SELECT, if you sign up with a reputable email marketing service, you'll be able to send messages to everyone on your list quickly and almost effortlessly. Some of these messages will be in the form of newsletters or event announcements. However, sometimes you'll want to set up a series of messages to go out to your list automatically, in a particular order and at a time of your choosing. This function is called an 'auto-responder.' With auto-responders, you write the messages any time you want, but they are delivered automatically at the time of your choosing.

One way to use an auto-responder is at the time a new person signs up for your mailing list. You can have a pre-programmed 'Welcome' message ready to go. You can set it up with your email provider so that, as soon as a new address arrives from someone who's claimed your free lead magnet, a welcome message goes out to her right away, without you lifting a finger. The welcome message is a typical use of the auto-responder function, but there are many others. Once you become familiar with how it works, you can become a much more effective email marketer.

Can you build this yourself? I sometimes make my own e-books and lead pages, but the learning curve was considerable! If you do something simple like a list or report you can deliver electronically, you can make your lead magnet in a word processing program such as WORD or Pages, and then save it as a PDF file. If you want to do something more elaborate or to make it more beautiful than what you can accomplish through word processing, use a design program instead. My favorite one is a free service called Canva. Canva is much easier to learn than, say, InDesign, the Adobe design program for professionals. They also have templates to help you get started.

Regarding landing pages, I don't recommend that you do this by yourself unless you have plenty of time, an eye for details and loads of patience with tech. You can subscribe to companies such as Lead Pages or Kajabi, each of which has a relatively hefty monthly cost attached. Each company provides tutorials on how to use their services, but they're difficult to follow for the novice. You can accomplish similar (but not as lovely) results with Mail Chimp for a much lower price, but it's still somewhat complicated the first few times you use it.

As far as your email marketing service is concerned, mastering the initial uses of Mail Chimp and Constant Contact (newsletter, database, auto-responder) are less daunting, but still a bit complex. A tutorial from your marketing coach or another specialist can set you on the right track to becoming independent so that you can build your email list without delay.

To see photo, design, email capture, and email marketing resources, visit the *Ways and Means* page at the end of our book. Life Force Marketing can also help you with each of the steps in email marketing.

Speaking Engagements

Speaking engagements are tailor-made for you IF you like to speak in front of groups. Even if you don't enjoy public speaking, but you realize that this could be a dynamite way for you to reach your tribe, I encourage you to lean into your growing edge and try it anyway. When you're the speaker, you're in charge of what you want to say. You'll probably have the freedom to tell your story in any way you desire. You'll have a chance to connect with new people. Many will feel they already know you by the end of your talk, and this can build trust.

If you have a book to sell or juicy handouts or samples, you can put them on a table in the room where you're speaking, either to sell or to give away. You can also ask for people's email addresses to participate in a drawing and conduct the drawing from the stage, thus growing your email list and adding some excitement to your program. For the drawing, give away a gift certificate to receive your services.

It takes time, thought, and research to find speaking opportunities that will put you in front of your Ideal Clients or potential referral partners. If you plan to do a lot of speaking, you may wish to develop what is sometimes called 'Your Signature Talk.' In this way, you develop a polished talk that includes all the points of the story you want to spread.

Can you build this yourself? Becoming an effective speaker is both a science and an art form and something that many people devote years to mastering. That doesn't mean you shouldn't jump in and give it a try as a means of promoting your business. If possible, enlist the support of someone who can provide you with feedback on both the content and the delivery of your talk before you go to your first engagement.

You'll find resources for improving your public speaking on our *Ways and Means* pages.

Newsletters

Newsletters come in myriad forms, including paper newsletters mailed out via the U.S. Post Office, and (more common these days) newsletters that are delivered electronically, usually to people on your email list. Creating electronic newsletters is easier now than ever before. Companies such as Constant Contact and Mail Chimp provide advanced technology, such as simple drag-and-drop templates, that make it relatively simple.

If you like to write, and if you have a flair for designing the written page, sending out a newsletter once a month or 4 times a year may be a good idea. Please note: Don't pack your newsletters with self-advertising. They should include a variety of ingredients such as short articles, images, quotes, interviews, relevant facts and statistics, or news about your joint venture partners.

Can you build this yourself? Again, I think you can figure this out yourself if you have a knack for it. However, if the writing and design, or the technical side of using the newsletter templates doesn't come quickly to you, get some help the first time and then you'll know how to do it on your own in the future. Forming a relationship with a local graphics designer is a good idea; she can be a godsend with your newsletters and in many other circumstances.

Self-Produced Events

Perhaps the services you provide can be translated into a group form such as a class, workshop, or retreat. Events can be simple one-hour affairs, once-weekly courses spread over a two-month period, or something that lasts for an entire week. Generally speaking, the shorter the event, the easier it is to produce. Often people are interested in your work but not ready to commit to a one-on-one relationship. A self-produced event can serve as an introduction and help grow your business.

No matter the length and complexity, there are a few things almost all successful events have in common. Most of what you do to create an event is done far in advance, and getting the timelines right will be a contributor to how well it goes:

- Decide on an appropriate venue that both appeals to, and is accessible to, your audience -- and is suitable for the activity you have in mind.
- Secure the venue for the date and time you want.
- Meet with the manager of the venue; learn about usage rules, where the bathrooms are, opening and closing procedures, costs and security deposits.
- Find out if the venue has a means of co-promoting your event.
- Decide on the content of your event – what experiences will you offer?
- Contact any collaborators or partners in advance to get on their calendars.
- Promote the event.
- Prepare any handouts that you'll be using.
- Rehearse or meet with your collaborators as you get closer to the event.
- Manage your registration.
- Send out follow-up messages.

Can you build this yourself? The difficulty varies with the length and complexity of the event. Offering a 2-hour introduction to Improving Posture through Bones for Life, Stress Relief for New Moms, or Professional Vocal Tips for Online Professionals, will be much easier than producing a week-long retreat on the same subject.

If this is your cup of tea, you can learn to do it. As with so many other marketing channels, if you're not sure how to proceed, get help the first time around and then plan to produce your future events independently. If you become very successful with live events, you can hire additional staff or a production company to take over many of the responsibilities.

As I've repeatedly said, build it if you want to, get help if you don't.

You may be the DIY type, but still, it's easy to get hooked on handing over part of your work load to others! Getting more help means you'll move faster.

My advice:
Give away as much of the work as you can afford, then focus on doing the things that ONLY you can do.

Here's something you can do right now.

- Which of the marketing channels that you've selected to spread the story of your private practice do you feel you could attempt on your own?
- What would you have to learn about to do the work yourself?
- Which of the marketing channels that you've selected seems to require some help to get started?
- Who might help you?
- Which kinds of professionals seem most important to add to your team?
- Do you know anyone in those professions already?
- Is there someone you trust who might be able to give you an educated recommendation?
- You may wish to use Life Force Marketing as a resource. To learn how, read the chapter: "How We Can Help: Life Force Marketing Services," or request a Complimentary Consultation.
- Celebrate how many choices you have and how much fun it will be to learn new things! Celebrate the new relationships you'll be forming to benefit your business!

part three

Energizing Your Presence in the World

Prosperity comes more easily when we
Enlist support wherever possible,
form good habits of Continuing, and
Celebrate every victory.

Enlist

Alone we can do so little;
together we can do so much.

Helen Keller

Enlist

Step 8
Enlist others to encourage and teach you and help keep you on track

By now you've realized that working toward your vision of the prosperous Life you want to live and the business you want to create will require you to grow in many ways both professionally and personally. You may even notice that this growth process has already begun just from doing a few of the exercises in our book or thinking through the ideas you've found here. Now let's devote a few minutes to considering something essential for the realization of your aspirations: The importance of having allies.

As we discussed earlier, there will be days when you experience self-doubt and disbelief in the viability of your Vision for yourself and your business. The inevitability of these negative influences is one reason why I recommend that you enlist the support of others to help you stay the course. You will also need allies to give you feedback, to provide accountability, to share additional information, to help with specific skills, and to offer high-level encouragement.

Show compassion for yourself! Enlist supporters. That's what this chapter is all about.

There are four main categories of people you can enlist to support you:

- Friends and Family
- A Marketing Coach
- Colleagues and Mastermind Partners
- Vendors with Specific Skills

Friends and Family

If you already have a supportive group of friends and family who will stand beside you through thick and thin, you are one of the fortunate ones. Count your blessings!

The people closest to you are an important resource; these folks can be your stalwart shoulders to lean on, those who will love you no matter what you do. They'll come to your events, tell their friends about your services, brag about you and, to some degree, listen to you talk about everything you're trying to do and the frustrations you're encountering along the way.

However, don't necessarily count on them to give you honest, constructive criticism or good relevant advice. They may not be comfortable in that role and might also lack the relevant knowledge to make substantive contributions to your progress. They possibly won't understand or be interested in the details of your work and your challenges.

It's also possible that some of your friends or family members don't fully believe in the viability of your Vision. At times you may have to avoid the topic of your Vision in the company of particular friends or family members who would try to discourage you or talk you out of attempting to live the Life you want to live.

A Marketing Coach

Of the four categories of people you can enlist for support, the most versatile – and perhaps the one most invested in your success -- is a marketing coach.

This kind of coach can provide you with comprehensive support every step of the way. He or she can work with you on defining your Vision and forming new habits about the stories you tell yourself. She can help you see how your unique resources provide invaluable elements. She can share smart, relevant feedback because she's gone through what you're going through many times before. She can not only help you define your Ideal Client and compose your stories, she can also help you select the best marketing channels and either build them with you or help you find other professionals to do so. She can also teach you to become more independent, if that's what you prefer, so that you don't have to rely on others in the future.

A marketing coach is someone who doesn't just tell you what needs to be done but shows you how, by partnering, mentoring, teaching, and modeling.

With a marketing coach, you can have someone standing beside you who will understand the Vision you're going for. She or he can provide both encouragement and salient suggestions to make your task much easier.

She can help you move through the areas of marketing you find especially challenging. She can be a mirror for you, giving you honest feedback about everything you're doing -- and supporting you as you remain excited about and committed to your Vision. She can help you avoid expensive and frustrating mistakes. She can help you discover the next steps to take, and in what order.

I wish I could have had an affordable hands-on, one-on-one marketing coach while I was learning about marketing myself. I was, instead, investing in group courses, reading books, and attending live events. It was a big relief when I met a one-on-one coach who was right for me. (Little known secret: almost all coaches have coaches because we know how indispensable they are).

Before finding a coach, I built a complete overall picture of the micro-business marketing process for myself through years of trial and error. It was a laborious, lengthy, expensive, and frustrating process to put it all together one piece at a time. I don't recommend that for you.

If I had found a marketing coach earlier in my career, I could have enlisted her help with a multitude of vexing problems. There were SO many times I would have loved to have a knowledgeable person to call for advice when I was facing a new direction or making a marketing decision! I surely would have had more financial success much sooner. I love having someone to call on who knows the terrain better than I because she's five steps ahead of me.

If you decide to hitch your wagon to a good marketing coach, and you do the work diligently and sincerely, your investment will come back to you multiplied in value.

You can increase your productivity, Vision and earning capacity. A marketing coach is uniquely suited to help you build the business of your dreams.

Colleagues and Mastermind Partners

The notion of the "mastermind" originally came from Napoleon Hill in his book *Think and Grow Rich.* His book was a landmark study of highly successful people. Participating in a mastermind is one of the 16 attributes that Hill observed in people who have amassed vast fortunes. As Hill himself put it, a mastermind group is:

> "The coordination of knowledge and effort of two or more people, who work toward a definite purpose, in the spirit of harmony."

According to Stephanie Burns in her 2013 article in Forbes Magazine

> "A mastermind group is designed to help you navigate through challenges using the collective intelligence of others... How does a mastermind work? A group of smart people meets weekly, monthly, even daily if it makes sense, to tackle challenges and problems together. They lean on each other, give advice, share connections and do business with each other when appropriate. It's peer-to-peer mentoring, and if you are lucky enough to get invited to one, you will most likely see a marked change in yourself and your business."

Being a member of a well-run mastermind group brings many benefits, including mutual support, new friendships, inspiration, motivation, differing perspectives, access to the resources of everyone in the group, and accountability.

Again, if you are already a member of a mastermind group or have a tight group of colleagues you can confide in, yahoo for you! You're way ahead of the curve.

Depending on the type of group you're in and the people you're partnering with, this could be a viable source of encouragement when you're feeling down, need advice or want a pal to help you celebrate.

They may be willing to hear you out when you describe the action steps you're taking and the goals you're trying to achieve. They may have had similar experiences and thus be able to offer answers to your questions. Some mastermind groups provide an accountability mechanism, so there's someone there to say, "Good for you! You finished working on your Ideal Client as you planned! You attended your first networking event and met three new potential clients there! You scheduled two Complimentary Consultations this week! You completed your Bio Statement! Let's hear all about it!"

Don't underestimate the power of this kind of informed encouragement! It's invaluable.

Finding a mastermind group that's right for you can take some trial and error. If you work with an expert or marketing coach, by all means, ask if they offer a mastermind program.

Life Force Marketing organizes mastermind groups. To learn more, see the *How We Can Help* page in the back of our book

If you enjoy being the initiator, you can start a group yourself! There are numerous existing templates for how a mastermind group might operate. You can learn more about starting a mastermind group; see the listing from LifeHack in the *Ways and Means* pages at the end of our book.

Vendors with Specific Skills

As we discussed in a previous chapter, Step 7: BUILD, vendors, and professionals with particular skill sets are almost a necessity in the process of marketing your services. Unless you have the necessary skills, or you plan to acquire them, you'll need someone to help you with a website, setting up your email database, or perhaps with some of your writing tasks.

You can hire an experienced social media marketer to teach you how to assemble and optimize a Facebook page or Linked In profile. If you have decided to produce a brochure, business cards, posters or information booklets, a graphic designer can be your new best friend. You will almost certainly need a printing company. If you struggle with getting your marketing language into compelling form, bringing a writer on board may be advisable. If you need a guide to help figure out the various websites you can use for photo, editing and design services, professional help from someone who's tech-savvy will provide a kickstart.

Vendors can be invaluable sources of suggestions and feedback on particular aspects of what you're doing. By all means think of them as members of your team, even if temporarily.

Here's something you can do right now.

- Take a few minutes and think about the family, friends, colleagues, and vendors in your life who could be supportive of your Vision.

- Imagine the specific kinds of support you might ask of them. For instance, you might ask your sister if she's willing to listen to you talk about your progress for an hour once a month. You could ask a colleague if he could meet with you every other week for early morning coffee to compare notes on each other's businesses.

- If there's someone you can call and approach directly, set an appointment for a conversation so you can talk to them and make your request.

- Set the location and time of your conversation; do your best to avoid interruptions.

- If you'd like to consider working with a marketing coach, set an appointment with someone you already know, or request a complimentary consultation with Life Force Marketing.

- Celebrate every victory! Celebrate the supportive people in your Life. Celebrate how far you've come, how much you've learned, by making it all the way through Step 8.

"Regardless of how you decide to proceed, please don't make the mistake of thinking you can do this all alone."

Mary Morrissey

Continue

The best way to predict your future
is to create it.

Abraham Lincoln

Continue

Step 9
Continue to Follow-up, Look Forward, Monitor, Listen, Envision and Revise

'CONTINUE' is the longest-lasting step of the ten. Continuing goes on indefinitely as long as you're building your practice. Even after your business is well established and attracting a steady flow of clientele, still, you continue, although your actual marketing activities may change in content, quantity or frequency.

After you've prepared yourself, your message and your marketing channels to notify your tribe about what you do -- after you've put all that in place -- that's when the ongoing work begins. That's when you practice a few skills until you become adept: following-up, looking forward, monitoring, listening, envisioning and revising. That's the crucible in which you continue to grow.

This chapter will outline a few of the particulars to help you think ahead.

Now it's time to WORK your system, stay connected to your strategic plan, answer the emails, give the talks, write the blog posts, listen to your potential new clients, monitor your progress, make changes when needed. Now is when you keep up your inner work around the story you tell yourself about yourself, interrupt the voice of the status quo, practice the NEDS process, persist on the days when you don't feel like it, and optimize your frame of mood as needed. Now is when you send out your scheduled social media posts, follow-up with everyone who came to your Open House.

It's time to work your plan. Here are a few pointers to help you stay the course.

Continue to Follow-Up

It's been said so often it's a cliché, and yet it's perfectly true: The fortune is in the follow-up. While you're moving toward your Vision, you're building momentum. You're creating a noticeable presence for yourself. As a result, you'll be starting up a whole slew of conversations with potential new clients!!

If you master follow-up, you're almost sure to flourish.

You will need a system to keep track of these potential new clients, their contact information, and the conversations you're having with them. Some people use old-fashioned index file cards or tickler files. Others use online sources. I've listed a few of these online providers, known as Contact Management Systems (CMS), in the *Ways and Means* chapter.

Some people create a spreadsheet or table chart to keep track of their potential new clients.

However you decide to do so…

You must keep track of the new people you meet, the phone calls you make, the emails you send, what has transpired with each person, and what needs to happen next.

Whatever you've decided needs to happen next goes on your calendar or To Do List!

If you say, "I'll call you next Thursday; we'll discuss details," put the call on your calendar as an appointment and make the call. This is a promise, and if you keep your promises, people will start to trust you. Every promise you make is a chance to deepen a relationship.

When you stay on top of the details in the follow-up process, you'll give a boost to your momentum, and you'll feel proud of yourself! You'll be rewarded for your consistency with a steady flow of business.

Continue to Look Forward, Be Prepared for Anything

One of the best things about being in business for yourself is that you can get in a flow of your own choosing. After a while, you'll know what to expect. You'll start having the feeling that you know what you're doing. It's satisfying to arrive at this point.

Still, from time to time, something unexpected will appear on the horizon. You may appreciate the surprising developments that will come your way – or you might feel thrown off balance as a result.

What might those developments look like?

You could become busy very quickly. How would you handle that? Are you prepared to adjust your business model or raise your prices, take on more clients or a partner, spend less time with each client or begin working more with groups? Being busy would be a lovely problem to have, and it's one that you don't want to overlook. It is a distinct possibility.

What if nothing seems to be working and no-one is calling you? Then it's time to revisit the basics. Ask yourself: Do my potential clients feel strongly enough about their problem that they'll spend money to solve it? Sharpen and refresh your vision. Revisit your Ideal Client profile. Are you speaking her language? Are you talking to her in the words she might use herself? Are there better ways to find your tribe? Do you need to scrap one of your chosen channels of spreading your stories and try something else? Should you enlist more help from someone with more experience or a different skill set?

Don't be surprised if adjustments are needed; some trial and error is to be expected. You can handle that! Just continue to have faith in yourself and you will be able to meet the occasional inevitable challenges.

Continue to Monitor Your Progress

Do you remember when you started out, when you were first acquiring the skills you use now in your professional life? Perhaps you attended classes in a university fine arts or art therapy department or a massage school; a Feldenkrais, Bones for Life, or Rolfing training; an energy medicine school; or a Health Coach training program. Maybe you endured the rigors of a Five Elements acupuncture program, one of Upledger's offerings, or a school of naturopathy. You may have studied with a master shaman, master life coach, or intuitive healer.

It's probably taken you years of practice to get good at what you do, especially if your work is in the arts or healing arts.

Whatever the path you've followed to become skillful at what you do, along the way you probably also developed another skill – one that's hidden from view. To get where you are now, you have grown a mental faculty for checking on your progress, whether consciously or unconsciously. At times, you've received grades from educators who reported how well you were doing, but your own internal progress monitor is probably more accurate than the formal evaluations. You know when your work is good, when it's getting better, and when it's slipping. You know when your clients are satisfied and when they're not. In other words, as you learned your craft, you also perfected your ability to monitor your progress, even if you weren't conscious of it.

Now it's time to apply that self-monitoring instinct of yours to monitoring your marketing progress.

Some of this evaluation happens intuitively.

However, much can also be done quantitatively. For instance, you can ask: Are you getting a steady flow of clients? How often does new business come your way? How long do your clients stick around? What percentage complete their programs with you? Do you have more income flowing your way now than you did in the past?

There are other aspects of your marketing that can be monitored using numbers.

For example, if you have an Open House, you can keep track of how much time you spend preparing, how many people you invite, how many attend, which of them brings a friend or signs up for a private session or class.

If you're paying for Facebook or Google ads, you can keep track of how many inquiries you receive per dollar spent, and to which ads people seem to respond most positively. If you send out postcards to people's home addresses, you can keep track of how many you send out, how much you spend on that effort, and how many new inquiries you receive as a result.

There are various ways of monitoring your online activity, too.

For instance, if you have a website, Google Analytics can show you the number of unique visitors your website had last week, as well as which parts of the world your visitors came from, and which websites referred them to you. Pretty cool! Website monitoring can shed a light on your online efforts and sometimes yield surprising information.

A note: Website analytics is a very technical subject. There are online companies who will gladly charge you whopping fees to drill down into analytics with you, the super geeks of what's called "traffic." I don't recommend you get caught up in it unless you're trying to build a national presence or be at the top of page one in a Google search; however, getting just the *basic* information from Google is free, fun and eye-opening.

On the more practical, less geeky side, mail marketing services, such as Constant Contact or Mail Chimp, can show you how many people opened your last newsletter, what percentage of people clicked on the links in your email, and several other things. These companies will routinely make reports available to help you know which articles, images and links are creating a positive audience response. For instance, I learned from a series of recent emails that the one that was opened most frequently had the word "video" in the subject line. Who knew? Also, the reports I received showed me that a high percentage of people who opened that email even clicked on the video link and, presumably, watched my video! (I guess I'll be making more videos... ☺)

There are many other sources of feedback that can help you hone in on your most effective marketing methods. If you can begin to sense which methods are working the best for you, you'll know where to focus your time and resources, and what to discontinue.

Here's an example:

REVELATIONS: Keeping track can reveal new insights

One of the things I do for pleasure is operate a boutique greeting card company that I started two years ago. The greeting card business is fun for me because I enjoy designing new cards and sharing them with people. My cards are mainly sold in local stores and at exhibits and other live events. Occasionally I hold an Open House to share new designs with people who live in the region. Recently I implemented a simple pen-and-paper tracking system for one of my Open Houses that yielded surprising results. I tallied who and how many people I invited, who attended, how many cards they bought, which cards each person purchased, which new designs they voted for, and whether they'd attended a previous Open House. One of the many things I learned is that, in offering around 100 card designs that day, the cards sold were not from just a few 'hot item' designs as I had suspected. Rather, my guests purchased over 47 different designs. I was tickled to learn that! Practically speaking, it means that my card designs have a broad appeal to people with diverse tastes and I should continue displaying a wide range of designs at my Open Houses.

Continue to Listen to Your Clients

Listening to clients is an area where people like us have a strategic advantage. We have an advantage because we work with clients one-on-one, because we may have given a lot of thought to our Intake and interview processes, and because we already have a habit of listening.

I hope that one of the things you take away from reading our book is an understanding of how important it is to listen to your clients very thoughtfully, and to 'read between the lines.' Listen to your current clients! They are your best sources for useful research!

When your clients are filling out your Intake Form, and you're interviewing them, listen for more than the facts. Listen, also, for the emotion they're communicating. Ask inquiring questions that go a little deeper to understand not only what they're experiencing, but what impact it's having on their Life. Revisit Step 5: COMPOSE to remind yourself how important it is to speak the language of your clients and to know the pain that their difficulties are causing.

The more you know about how your clients are feeling, the more you'll understand them. The more you can speak their language and show you know what their day-to-day experience is like, the more you'll be able to write and talk in ways that say, "I'm the person who can assist you."

In short, when your Ideal Clients come into contact with you in person, in print, on the airwaves, at an event, or online, you must be speaking their language.

As your business grows, listening to your clients will also yield other valuable information. You'll learn which of your services is helping people the most, and how much support they need.

They may request changes in your business that you hadn't considered! They may ask for an option to purchase a "package deal" from you. Or they may even ask you to provide a new service or product that you haven't thought of or offered before.

Continue to Envision and Revise Your Inner Story

Although I promise you, there will be days you feel like doing so -- don't give up on a new story for yourself! Keep your Vision top of mind.

As you undoubtedly already know, re-inventing yourself, even just a little bit, is a conscious act of creation, and one that requires consistent, sustained attention.

Mary Morrissey often asks the assembled crowds of 800+ attendees at her Dreambuilder Live events:

> "How often should you revisit your Vision?"
>
> And the crowd answers with one booming voice: "EVERY DAY!"
> Yes. Every. Single. Day.

And that also applies to the techniques you learned in Step 2: REVISE. Keep those practices alive in yourself by practicing them (or something similar). Make a habit of using the NEDS process. Notice what you're feeding with your attention. These practices will become your cherished allies.

Continuing Is Where the Rubber Meets the Proverbial Road.

When your Vision seems blurry or too far away, when you've worked hard but still don't have the results you want, when you lose a client, are faced with setbacks and obstacles -- Continuing is the phase of your business when you keep going, repeating your best practices, renewing your belief in yourself again, and then again.

This is when you either persevere or give up.

This is when you keep your Vision fresh or allow your current bossy paradigm to keep you stuck in an old cage.

This is when you watch and listen, continue to learn and innovate, consult your inner guidance.

This is when you reinvent yourself and move daily toward your Vision.

This is when you try different things, keep learning, and see what works.

This is when you lean in on the people you've enlisted to support you.

This is when you celebrate every victory.

As you continue you will be met with new challenges on a regular basis; that's inevitable as you and your business simultaneously grow.

This is when you remind yourself, as often as necessary, "I can do this. I can do this!"

Continuing Can Also Lead to New Opportunities

At the beginning of our book, we talked a lot about Life Force, the invisible force that animates all of nature. Although the practices and habits you'll be developing and strengthening as you Continue may seem practical on the surface, they also have a deeper meaning and impact.

When you Continue in thoughtful ways, you repeatedly broadcast your intentions to the Universe. There's power in action that's based on belief. As you continue to grow stronger, and so will your business. It's inevitable that, eventually, the word will spread about the great work you're doing.

As your story spreads, you may have other service providers offer to partner with you or form joint ventures. You may be asked to come and speak to a group of people who are interested in what you're doing and who you are.

You may outgrow some of your ways of doing business or even your location. If you're a home-based person, you may decide it's time to move into a commercial environment or share space with other like-minded providers. You may receive an offer to do your work in another city or state.

One way or the other, Life is likely to become increasingly interesting.

A Few Additional Gentle Reminders...

- Remember that you're in this for yourself and others.
- Revisit your Vision DAILY and bring it up to date at least once a month.
- Listen to your favorite inspirational teachers in person or on video to keep your frame of mood where you want it to be.
- Minimize your exposure to negative news and people.
- Ask for support from your coach or mastermind partners.
- Be patient with yourself.
- Do nurturing, affirming, pleasing things for yourself on a daily basis.
- Give yourself time to develop new manifesting muscles.
- Smell the roses, inhale beauty.
- Practice Gratitude, especially for your current clients.
- Celebrate every victory!

Here's something you can do right now.

Practice keeping track of the new people you meet, the phone calls you make, what has transpired with each person and what needs to happen next by doing the following exercise:

- Visit Insightly.com, which is one of the Contact Management Systems you can use to help keep track of your potential clients.
- Investigate their terms and sign up for a free trial.
- Enter names of a few friends to use as guinea pigs so you can see how Insightly works.
- Add their contact information.
- Contact one or two of these friends, either by phone or email. Tell them you're practicing using a new system and you want to practice keeping track of the conversations you have. Enter the information about this phone call or email contact in Insightly.
- Set an appointment for your next call or email. Put the date on your calendar and enter it in Insightly.
- Follow-up by making the call or sending the email at the appointed time.
- Celebrate every victory! Celebrate your investigation of a contact management system! By this time, you probably don't even need my suggestions! I imagine you're getting good at finding things to celebrate.

If you don't like the idea of doing this electronically for any reason, visit our website to learn about Tickler Files: LifeForceMarketing.com/MORE

Celebrate!

I just want to celebrate another day of livin'
I just want to celebrate another day of Life!

Rare Earth

Celebrate!

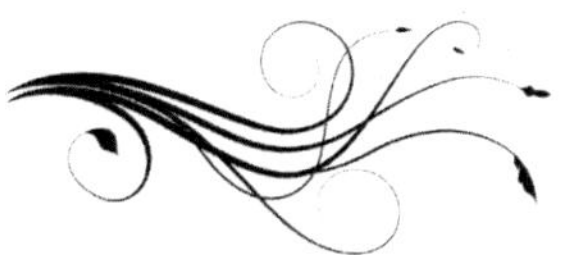

Step 10
Celebrate Every Victory!

I believe that by now I've made it clear: Celebrating your victories, large and small, is of paramount importance. Building a business is a marathon, not a sprint. If you don't celebrate each lap, you won't have the mental stamina to get to the finish line. To succeed in creating your Vision, you must find a reliable way to maintain a positive mindset. Celebrating each victory may be the single best way of preserving that mindset over time. There are many excellent reasons to make celebrating a habit.

Because if you don't celebrate every victory...

- You may have a tendency to negate your successes.
- You may get horn-swaggled or distracted by demoralizing thoughts.
- You may not notice tiny bits of progress creeping in and building up steam.
- You might sabotage yourself by deciding you're tired of the whole process.
- Someone will discourage you, and you'll lack the Mo-Jo to fight back.

And if you do celebrate every victory...

- Celebrating every bit of progress builds up a beautiful vibrating frequency in your energy field that will continue to attract more of the same.
- Looking for ways to celebrate will be an excellent exercise for your imagination.
- You'll generally become a happier person.
- This habit will become contagious, and you will effortlessly pass it along to your clients and loved ones.

How might you celebrate your victories?

That's entirely up to you. Celebrating is a personal thing.
You could:
get some extra sleep
listen to your favorite music
call your best friend
buy someone a present
have a few friends over for a glass of wine
read your favorite poet
give yourself a day off to do anything you want
do something naughty and laugh the entire time
plant flowers
paint your face
put a blue streak in your hair
get a pedicure
pay someone else to clean your house
put a message in a bottle and bury it as a time capsule
throw away a bunch of clothes you don't like anymore
go for a bike ride
plan a vacation
crawl into bed with an excellent novel
watch your favorite comedian
have a hot fudge sundae
put balloons or fresh flowers all over your house
buy a new outfit
take yourself out to a fancy restaurant
do something special with your sweetheart or your mom
finally do that thing you've wanted to do for all these years
spend time at an art gallery
throw a luau
rent a pontoon boat for the weekend
swing from a grapevine…
it's really up to you.

Just do it!
Just do it!
Just do it!

What would you say constitutes a victory?

That's up to you, too, but here are a few suggestions:

- Completing a "*Here's something you can do right now*" activity from one of the chapters in our book
- Feeling new inspiration for a Vision of the Life you'd love to live
- Writing down or otherwise documenting your Vision
- Reaching a milestone in any new, intentionally created habit
- Solving the puzzle of Who is your Ideal Client
- Attending your first networking event
- Having an AHA! moment about how marketing is something you can do
- Finding someone to support your belief in your Vision
- Enlisting a new vendor to help you out
- Hiring a marketing coach
- Receiving a referral!
- Coming up with a dynamite elevator speech
- Finding the perfect image for your website or designing a new logo
- Buying your domain name
- Scheduling a live event
- Putting up a new page on your website
- Choosing a new marketing approach and getting some help to make it a reality
- Approaching a potential joint venture partner
- Talking to someone who's interested in your services
- Meeting a new client!
- Meeting another new client!

Cheers! **Opah!** *Yahoo!*

Mazaltov! Bravo! Yippee!

Visit our site for a link to my favorite dance soundtrack on YouTube! LifeForceMarketing.com/MORE

My favorite ways to celebrate

watching haute couture runway shows online
planning an exotic vacation, finding very chill places to stay
walking in my garden or doing nothing at all on a rainy day
spending the day drawing and painting just for fun
lying on the floor and doing a Feldenkrais lesson
having lunch or a glass of wine with a friend
enjoying a banana split or receiving a pedicure
hiring helpers to do almost anything for me that I usually do myself!
going for a ride in the country on my Genuine Buddy Scooter
sharing the celebration with my son, my mom, friends or siblings
luxuriating in a long shower while singing at the top of my lungs!
dancing or hanging out in the pool with my granddaughter
hopping over to an art gallery or buying a new pair of earrings
buying a bunch of flowers and creating an outrageous arrangement
watching the antics of the birds, butterflies, and bunnies in my backyard
swimming or wading in, floating or boating on any body of water
going to Maui for a month
pounding my chest and making Tarzan noises ☺

Celebrate Every Victory !

part four

Additional Sparks

How We Can Help

Services Provided by Life Force Marketing.

20 specialized coaching packages for every business stage, from beginner to veteran

LIFT OFF, 20 coaching sessions

Following and expanding upon the 10 Steps of Holistic Marketing. Meriah helps your new practice achieve lift off in record time; we'll help you light the fire and keep the flame burning.

Part One: Igniting the Fires of Intention, 6 coaching sessions
Welcome to self-employment! Flesh out your Vision, limiting beliefs, and all the resources that can contribute to your success.

Part Two: Initiating Vital Actions, 10 coaching sessions
Start attracting clients! Choose your niche and Ideal Client, explore their problems. Discover where to find your Ideal Client, compose your marketing language, select several marketing channels.

Part Three: Energizing Your Presence in the World, 4 coaching sessions
Put your plans in motion! Enlist support, learn fine points of continuing.

INVIGORATE, 16 coaching sessions

Liven up your existing practice, take steps to fulfill its potential. Meriah will help you build on what you've already done, create new momentum -- and then increase your velocity.

Part One: Begin with What You Already Have, 4 coaching sessions
Build on everything you've already done! Clarify next steps, update your Vision, revise limiting beliefs, escalate use of your current resources.

Part Two: Narrow Your Focus, 10 coaching sessions
Go deeper than you've gone before... Expand understanding of your niche, Ideal Client, their problems. Discover where to find Ideal Client, compose your marketing language, reconsider your chosen marketing channels.

Part Three: Hit the Restart Button, 2 coaching sessions
Take your business to new heights! Enlist support, dig into the finer points of continuing. Commit to celebrating victory as a habit.

YOUR CLIENT CORNUCOPIA, 10 coaching sessions

If you've already done your Envisioning work and written your Resource List, this may be for you. Work with Meriah and her team to:

- Define your niche and Ideal Client
- Learn, or review, the basics of client attraction, enrollment and follow-up
- Compose your five marketing stories
- Revise your beliefs
- Keep your clients coming back for more

ESTABLISH & EXPAND your online presence, 14 coaching sessions

If you already know your Ideal Client, have a well-developed Vision, and have made a thorough Resource list, Meriah can help you use all that advance work to your advantage. Expect to:

- Examine your current online presence for clues and analysis
- Revise your stories, address your brand
- Grow your email list, lead magnets, lead pages and more
- Explore other online options; choose your online venues.
- Determine the kind of community you want to build
- Get the assistance you need to build your marketing channels

DEVELOP, PRODUCE, and PROMOTE your "Hot Topic" Local Event, 8 coaching sessions

If you know your Ideal Client, have started Composing your 5 Stories, and have a clear Vision, Meriah will huddle with you to:

- Choose your Hot Topic
- Write your Resource list
- Revise your stories, reveal your brand
- Promote, produce and monitor your local event

SHINE A SPOTLIGHT, 4 coaching sessions each

Our short-term coaching plans shine a bright light on specific elements of your marketing process. If you want to focus on a narrow area of your marketing process, Meriah will jump in with you in any of the following areas:

Anyone, at any stage of business, can select from the following topics:

- Ignite Your Powerful Vision
- More Fire in the Belly: Energizing Your Self-Confidence

- Choose an Ideal Client
- Keep Track of Your Prospects
- Get Started with Email Marketing

more SHINE A SPOTLIGHT choices, 4 coaching sessions each

If you already know your Ideal Client, these topics are also open to you:

- Compose Your Compelling Stories
- Your First Exhibit
- Your First Newsletter
- Your Client Enrollment Conversation
- Select Your Marketing Channels
- Inspire Loyalty in Your Clients: Improve Your Client Retention
- *Two-part topics: Choose 101 or 202, or both*
    - Revise Your Story, Reveal Your Brand 101
    - Revise Your Story, Reveal Your Brand 202
    - Fortune Hunting: Perfect Your Follow-Up 101
    - Fortune Hunting: Perfect Your Follow-Up 202
    - Grow your Email List 101
    - Grow your Email List 202
    - Develop Your Signature Talk 101
    - Develop Your Signature Talk 202

MASTER MIND GROUPS

We are in the process of forming new master mind groups. Please contact us if you would like to learn more or be added to a waiting list.

If you'd like to talk about which coaching program might work best for you, you're invited to request a Complimentary Consultation at:

www.LifeForceMarketing.com/CONTACT

How to Request
a Complimentary Consultation

I hope that reading *Life Force Marketing* has inspired you and given you a bushel basket full of practical insights for building your business. Whether you're expanding your existing practice, striking out on your own after being part of a group, or starting something new totally from scratch, the same principles apply.

If, after reading these chapters, you feel a rush of optimism and curiosity, a good feeling that "maybe I can do this," then I invite you to schedule a complimentary consultation with me.

You may be wondering, what is a Complimentary Consultation? Good question. Here's how it goes:

We'll meet in person, by phone, Skype or Zoom for about 45 minutes.

The flow of the conversation will reflect what you've read here. I'll ask about your Vision, what you want to achieve, and what gets in your way. There will be plenty of time to get your questions answered.

From there I'll make a recommendation. Based on what I've learned about you, I'll share next steps you might take, whether we should consider taking some of the steps together, and, if so, how to begin. If I don't think we're a perfect fit, I may refer you to someone else.

You'll receive insights about next steps for your business whether we decide to work together or not!

Your Complimentary Consultation will not be a sales pitch on my part. There's no obligation for you to enroll in any of my programs.

I can't wait to hear from you and see how we might work together to help bring your Prosperity Vision into reality!

Meriah Kruse

www.LifeForceMarketing.com/CONTACT

Origins
of Life Force Marketing

The vision-based holistic approach to marketing I'm sharing with you here is a distillation of what I've learned and applied during 35 years of leadership in for-profit and non-profit enterprises and projects. Many of these enterprises were of my own invention. I've learned a lot about marketing along the way, especially for one-person and very small businesses.

Not surprisingly, as the daughter of two entrepreneurial fathers (no, that's not a misprint!), my own foray into self-employment began young, hemming coats for my dormitory girlfriends at the University of Kentucky when I was 17. Next in line was operating a cleaning and painting service in California with a partner. Venturing into the non-profit world a few years later, I helped pioneer two tiny dance organizations, each of which quickly sprouted into statewide forces in the Arts — one in California and one in Kentucky. That's how my marketing initiation began in earnest.

Later, I completed a training program at the International Professional School of Bodywork in San Diego. When first starting out as a massage therapist, I was in the same position many of you are in; having something profound to offer, but not knowing how to spread the word. Fortunately, I had a successful massage practice that supported my son and me for many years. I worked for five years in multi-therapist wellness centers; the rest of the time I practiced out of my home.

After five years in therapeutic massage, I became a Guild Certified Feldenkrais Practitioner. The challenges of building a practice in that field were even more daunting than massage therapy because no one in my community knew what the Feldenkrais Method was! I had to develop new marketing chops and try new approaches. After ten years in Feldenkrais, I added Bones for Life to my menu of modalities.

In addition to 25 years of operating a wellness practice, I founded and operated an adventure travel company, Gentle Adventure Retreats for Women. This was my first foray into internet marketing. I also hosted innumerable workshops, festivals, seminars, and performances, and collaborated with other practitioners and artists in venues ranging from parks to university classrooms and exotic retreat centers. Along the way, I continued to learn about marketing for micro-businesses.

When the internet ascended to prominence, so did a new type of entrepreneur: the internet-based coach. I enrolled in online trainings with some of the most accomplished marketing wizards in North America. I read their books, attended their live events, webinars and online coaching sessions, spent thousands of dollars on my marketing education, hired consultants, and then used it all to build my own businesses.

My journey has included founding, marketing and/or managing:

- A 15-year career as a dancer, choreographer, producer and arts administrator;
- Several forays into network marketing, most successfully with ASEA Cellular Health, where I played a role in ushering over 1,000 people into new businesses;
- Launching and building a 25-year holistic practice, emphasizing massage therapy, the Feldenkrais Method of Movement Education and Bones for Life;
- A few of the programs I launched and operated: Women on the Move, Optimistic Aging, Alive on WHEELS, Be Free to Move
- Founding an adventure travel company in which I led groups of women, and sometimes men, to Maui, Mexico, South Carolina and Kentucky.
- Founding Good Tidings Greeting Cards, Kentucky's only full-service greeting card company, incorporating my original designs.

Most recently, I've opened the doors to Life Force Marketing, a coaching, teaching and writing company dedicated to empowering holistic practitioners, service-oriented artists and retirees ready to start their own businesses. My journey has led me to the book that's in your hands. It's been a thrill so far!

Am I an expert in every area of marketing? Not by a long shot. I still study and learn about business, marketing, tech and design almost every day because it fascinates me. But my particular type of bootstrap journey of building micro-businesses has turned me into a versatile and relatively self-reliant solopreneur. I hope to pass that on to You!

The entire point of Life Force Marketing is to show you how you can engage your personal Life Force in a vital adventure: reaching the level of prosperity you imagine for your business or practice through a holistic type of marketing that you'll feel comfortable aligning yourself with and may even learn to enjoy.

In my opinion, you deserve it.

Wishing you every blessing, *Meriah Kruse*

Addendum:
Three Methods Worth Investigating for Revising the Stories You Tell Yourself about Yourself

You can find more information on our site
www.LifeForceMarketing.com/MORE

1
The Feldenkrais Method of Movement Education

Many people think of the Feldenkrais Method as something to fix posture, solve pain problems, or help recover from strokes or surgeries. It is those things, but more accurately, it's one of the most profound body-mind methods devised thus far by humankind. Although the lessons are largely physical in nature, the effects are multi-dimensional.

Made up of over 1,000 exploratory lessons involving movement and guided attention, this method creates changes in the stories we tell ourselves about ourselves by changing our felt sense of who we are.

By shifting your self-image, one lesson at a time, the body-mind infrastructure that supports your personal narratives is gradually rebuilt into something that more accurately reflects your current reality.

Dr. Moshe Feldenkrais, Ph.D., the physicist and martial artist who developed the method bearing his name, had many helpful things to say about self-image. Importantly for our purposes here, one thing he observed is that our self-image is continually evolving.

> "In reality our self-image is never static. It changes from action to action."
>
> *Dr. Moshe Feldenkrais, Ph.D.*

That's good news for us when we want to revise the stories we tell ourselves, take on new life challenges, or even completely reinvent ourselves if that's our choice.
This implies that in our natural state of affairs, no matter what our self-image is today, it will continue to evolve in accordance with our actions, thoughts and feelings.

However, there is an adversary to this natural evolution, and that adversary is Habit.

Much of the work for students of the Feldenkrais Method involves changing habits on both the conscious and the unconscious levels.

From 20 years' experience with these lessons I've discovered that we can literally change not only our self-images but also the meaning we attribute to the events in our past. With this also comes the ability to alter the futures we can imagine.

Although it's fascinating to write and talk about it, the Feldenkrais Method must be experienced to be adequately understood.

There are also additional Feldenkrais resources listed in the *Ways and Means* chapter at the end of this book and on our website.

2
The Work, by Byron Katie

As Byron Katie says on her website, thework.com

> "The Work is a simple yet powerful process of inquiry that teaches you to identify and question the thoughts that cause all the suffering in the world. It's a way to understand what's hurting you, and to address the cause of your problems with clarity."

Through the use of just four questions, Katie stimulates a re-thinking of the commitment to our own deeply held views about Life and our place in it.

The most impactful of these questions is "Who would I be without this thought?" Answering this question can be a moving and transformative experience.

Few systems of personal growth hold more promise for liberating Life Force than her four famous questions. I urge you to investigate them for yourself.

3
Quantum Life Changes

In January 2014, I took a ten-day trip to Cuenca, Ecuador to join Cardell and Lin Vermilion Smith, of Quantum Life Changes, for a personal retreat.

I had time and money on my hands and was looking for a Big Experience, something that would change my Life for the better, in a holistic way.

After many hours on the internet searching hither and yon, I discovered Quantum Life Changes. I soon realized that they were on a similar personal growth path as my own, but farther down the path than I. So, the three of us agreed that I would come to Ecuador and plunge into a personal retreat with them in their home in Cuenca.

And that original desire to do something that would change my Life for the better? It worked out just as I had hoped.

Their teachings drew from Byron Katie's work, the new evolving areas of neuro-science related to changing the brain, and from ancient wisdom teachings.

Rather than going into a lengthy discussion of the theories behind their work, I'd rather give you the opportunity to experience an exercise from their program. You can find this exercise on my website. www.LifeForceMarketing.com/WORK

I use the mental/spiritual exercises from Quantum Life Changes every day in my personal Life and my private coaching practice and I'm never disappointed with the results.

Ways and Means

Resources to Help You Take a Next Step...

our website:
www.LifeForceMarketing.com

our extended resource page:
www.LifeForceMarketing.com/MORE

Good Tidings Greeting Cards and Custom Cards
www.GoodTidingsCards.com

Meriah's ASEA Cellular Health website
www.AGoodLife.teamasea.com

Investigate some of the coaches and teachers whose work is quoted and referred to in our book:

Mary Morrissey, "Dreambuilder Toolkit"
www.marymorrissey.com
Denise Wakeman, "Visibility Lab," "Marketing Trailblazers"
www.denisewakeman.com
Jan Marie Dore
www.janmariedore.com
Marketing for Hippies, Tad Hargrave "Marketing Can Feel Good"
www.marketingforhippies.com
Bill Baren, "Client Enrollment Mastery"
www.billbaren.com
Allison Rapp, Hands-On Practitioner Coaching
www.allisonrapp.com
Ryan Eliason, "Visionary Business School"
www.visionarybusinessschool.com
Eben Pagan, "Grow Your Business, Profit and Income"
www.ebenpagantraining.com
Danny Iny, Mirasee, "Reimagine Business"
www.mirasee.com

Learn more about Linn and Cardell Smith, Quantum Life Changes
www.quantumlifechanges.com

Learn more about Byron Katie's "The Work"
Her primary website: www.thework.com

Learn more about the Feldenkrais Method:

Official site of the Feldenkrais Guild of North America: Feldenkrais.com
The International Feldenkrais Federation: Feldenkrais-method.org

Learn more about Bones for Life:

Official site of the Foundation for Movement Intelligence
www.movementintelligence.org

Learn to use your voice more confidently:

- Katie Bull, Whole Body/Whole Voice (group and individual voice classes in NY and remotely) www.katiebull.com

- Ed Desiato. www.Udemy.com/take-lessons-from-an-actor-speak-with-confidence-class

Purchase Feldenkrais videos, books or audios (alpha listing)

- Feldenkrais Resources, one of the country's oldest somatic education organizations and the publisher of Moshe Feldenkrais's audio legacy
    - www.feldenkraisresources.com

- Future Life Now, home of Cynthia Allen, Feldenkrais Practitioner and Bones for Life Trainer
    - www.futurelifenow.com

- Inside Moves, home of Jeff Haller, Feldenkrais Trainer
    - www.insidemoves.org

- Mind in Motion, home of Larry Goldfarb, Feldenkrais Trainer
    - www.mindinmotion-online.com

- The Feldenkrais Store
    - www.achievingexcellence.com

- The Journey Inward, home of Diane Razumny, Feldenkrais Trainer
    - www.feldenkraisjourney.com

- Uncommon Sensing, home of Alan Questel, Feldenkrais Trainer
    - www.uncommonsensing.com

Questions related to social media:
www.SocialMediaExaminer.com

Free online graphic design:
Canva www.canva.com

Free, high-resolution, professional photos online:
(Note: always give attribution – thank the photographer every chance you get!)
Unsplash www.Unsplash.com
Pexels www.pexels.com

Free online photo editing:
Pixlr www.pixlr.com

Email, newsletter, auto-responder programs:
Constant Contact www.constantcontact.com
MailChimp www.mailchimp.com

Email list-building strategies:
www.AmyPorterfield.com

Register new domain names and host your website:
GoDaddy www.godaddy.com
BlueHost www.bluehost.com
HostGator www.hostgator.com

Back up all your files in the cloud:
Carbonite www.carbonite.com

Contact Management Systems for tracking client conversations:
Insightly www.insightly.com
HubSpot (free) www.hubspot.com

Host, promote and sell online courses, and/or for hosting e-books for email capture all "under one roof":
Kajabi www.Kajabi.com
LeadPages www.Leadpages.net
Get Response www.Getresponse.com

An article about starting a mastermind group:
www.lifehack.org/articles/featured/how-to-start-and-run-a-mastermind-group.html

Learn more about ASEA Cellular Health:
Meriah Kruse's team website www.AGoodLife.teamasea.com

Listen to Rev. Michael Beckwith Sunday talks and archives:
Agape International Spiritual Center www.agapelive.com

Wishing you good fortune,
and a conscious relationship
with your sacred Life Force

Brooke with Maui Protea, Photo by Meriah Kruse

May all beings be free from suffering

Meriah Kruse

Balin Kruse-Williams

Life Force Marketing

www.LifeForceMarketing.com/CONTACT

Made in the USA
Columbia, SC
06 August 2022

64566143R00126